**DES** **ROFITS**

A successful design practice requires principals and staff who are creative, technically proficient, and financially savvy. *Designing Profits* focuses on the last component—the one that is so elusive for many architects, engineers, and construction professionals—the business aspects of practice.

Not an ordinary book on practice issues or finance, *Designing Profits* explains the application of design thinking to guide wise business decisions. It is indeed possible to be as creative in establishing and operating a practice as in designing and constructing a building. The book offers comprehensive guidance and objective tools that support design professionals to reap financial rewards from their practices and to discover innovative strategies to become entrepreneurial and implement creative practice models.

An extended case study is woven throughout the book. Witness the trials and tribulations of Michelangelo & Brunelleschi Architects as they encounter problematic clients, tight project budgets and schedules, low fees and insufficient profits, marketing issues, quirky staff, technology upgrades, and growth, among other difficult challenges. This mythical firm—a composite of several real-life practices—navigates through these various dilemmas, providing readers with insights into superior financial management and a reimagined services portfolio.

**Morris A. Nunes** is an attorney with over 30 years' experience as outside counsel for businesses and professional practices. He has served as Adjunct Professor at Georgetown University and Catholic University. He has written five previous books on business topics and holds a law degree from Georgetown and degrees from the University of Pennsylvania and its Wharton School of Business.

**Andrew Pressman**, FAIA, an architect, Professor Emeritus at the University of New Mexico, and Lecturer at the University of Maryland, leads his own award-winning architectural firm in Washington, DC. He has written numerous critically acclaimed books and articles, and he holds a master's degree from the Harvard University Graduate School of Design.

# DESIGNING PROFITS

## CREATIVE BUSINESS STRATEGIES FOR DESIGN PRACTICES

## MORRIS A. NUNES AND ANDREW PRESSMAN

Routledge
Taylor & Francis Group

LONDON AND NEW YORK

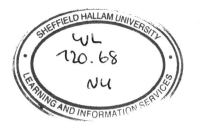

First published 2016
by Routledge
2 Park Square, Milton Park, Abingdon, Oxon OX14 4RN

and by Routledge
711 Third Avenue, New York, NY 10017

*Routledge is an imprint of the Taylor & Francis Group, an informa business*

*British Library Cataloguing-in-Publication Data*
A catalogue record for this book is available from the British Library

*Library of Congress Cataloging in Publication Data*
Nunes, Morris A., 1949– author.
    Designing profits : creative business strategies for design practices /
    Morris Nunes and Andrew Pressman.
        pages cm
    Includes bibliographical references and index.
    1. Architectural practice—Management. 2. Design services—
    Management. I. Pressman, Andy, author. II. Title.
    NA1996.N86 2016
    720.68—dc23                                          2015022301

ISBN: 978-1-138-83847-5 (hbk)
ISBN: 978-1-138-83848-2 (pbk)
ISBN: 978-1-315-73430-9 (ebk)

Typeset in Helvetica
by Keystroke, Station Road, Codsall, Wolverhampton

MIX
Paper from
responsible sources
FSC
www.fsc.org  **FSC® C013056**

Printed and bound in Great Britain by
TJ International Ltd, Padstow, Cornwall

## Morris A. (Maury) Nunes

With gratitude, I dedicate this book to the women who have been and are at the center of my life, all of whom have taught—and still teach—me so much:

My Grandmothers: Jennie Epstein Nunes and Mary Kaseno Ecoff

My Mother: Betty Ann Ecoff Nunes

My Late Wife: Jane Susan Chargar Nunes

My Wife: Ruth Lenora Peterson Warsoff Nunes

My Daughter: McKenzie Whitney Nunes

My Daughter-in-Law: Allison Truesdell Nunes

## Andrew Pressman

This is dedicated to Lisa whose support is unconditional and unwavering, and whose own practice issues and their resolution sparked many ideas contained herein. And to Samantha and Daniel who keep us alert with their intelligence, wit, and spirit.

# CONTENTS

# 3 ACCOUNTING: CREATING RELIABLE INPUTS AND OUTPUTS | 27

# 4 DATA APPLICATION: REFINING ANALYTICS AND CONTROLLING COSTS | 49

# 5 GROWTH AND ITS CONSTRAINTS: MAKING WISE CHOICES | 73

## 6 STRATEGIC FINANCIAL PLANNING: SETTING AND REACHING PROFIT TARGETS | 91

## 7 RETHINKING PRACTICE: TACTICAL INNOVATIONS FOR FINANCIAL PROSPERITY AND PROFESSIONAL SATISFACTION | 119

## 8 PROGRESS NOTES: WRAPPING UP AND MOVING FORWARD | 143

# FOREWORD

I first met one of the authors of *Designing Profits*, Andrew Pressman, when he and I were receiving our Fellowships in the American Institute of Architects (AIA). In addition to admiring each other's long, black, polyester robes, we both remarked on the plethora of old(er) white guys in our 2002 Fellowship group—along with its lack of diversity. Well, there has since been a gentle increase of the AIA's minority and women membership, so it makes sense that one of the two partners of the mythical design firm referred to in the book is Mary Michelangelo.

The book is not about Mary, or her partner Bob Brunelleschi; it's about understanding and improving the financial management of a design firm, and that information is critical to a firm's success. And by incorporating Mary, Bob, their staff, and advisors, the reader develops immediate identification with them, their firm—Michelangelo & Brunelleschi Architects (M&B)—and their business dilemmas. That technique does an excellent job of making the book more accessible and readable.

Co-authors Maury Nunes and Andrew Pressman note in the Preface that the typical college education does a poor job of teaching financial management skills to students of architecture, engineering, interior design, and construction management. *Designing Profits* serves the multiple purposes of providing that knowledge for students as well as for practicing architects and allied professionals.

The two major subjects described in the book—financial initiatives and performance initiatives—can result in more meaningful work and greater firm profitability.

■ *Financial initiative* addresses all the nuances of relevant accounting and financial management. It is not a primer for CPAs but it tackles all the financial components of a design firm. I wish I had had this book to hand out to my staff when they wanted to understand the difference between accrual and cash accounting or learn how to examine project profitability.

- **Performance initiative** is an outgrowth of superior financial management that can be achieved through the book's teachings. Specifically, measuring project performance and determining which project types are most effective for a firm allows the business to reimagine its services and portfolio. *Designing Profits* presents analytic techniques to determine the financial viability of a firm's jobs. In turn, that enables Mary and Bob to make practical business decisions regarding project types to pursue—or discontinue.

A crucial component of *Designing Profits* is clear from the title. It is not just another professional practice book on finances and accounting—it is about using design to improve your business. As the authors note, "designing (or redesigning) and operating a business should be as creative and compelling as designing and constructing a building."

I have always believed that business works hand in glove with design to create and grow, with an oft-repeated mantra of: "We are a business that does design. We are not a design business." This book provides strong explanations, and validation, of how focusing on the business is what enables a firm to produce superlative design work. It also helps put a design student and professional in the right frame of mind for collaborating with clients—understanding that an architect's role is to support the client's business through design. In other words, the business side is not a necessary evil—it is the very thing that allows design to happen.

Following that thought, a majority of architects feel that they are not compensated appropriately for their education and contribution to their clients' success. Complaining is not the way to solve that problem—absorbing the fundamentals of *Designing Profits* is. The book is distinguished from other business books because it provides *objective tools* and drills down to address the difficult issues. By using the analytics presented, it is a straightforward exercise to determine where your firm's financial management is working well and where it is not, even perhaps illuminating dark corners where it has not been working at all. Those objective tools allow financial modeling to investigate options—"what-ifs"—that can improve profit, and therefore compensation, dramatically.

When you first begin reading this book, you might feel intimidated because there are actually numbers, tables, and charts. But just as at one point you learned how to draw a perspective, you can learn from this book how to use creative business strategies that can make your practice more profitable—and more rewarding.

**Richard N. Pollack, FAIA, FIIDA**
Pollack Consulting | Richard@RichardNPollack.com

# PREFACE

**W**elcome to *Designing Profits: Creative Business Strategies for Design Practices.* This is the final book in the "Designing" trilogy, which also includes *Designing Architecture* and *Designing Relationships.* The distinctive message imparted by the trilogy is that the whole package—doing great design, getting it built, *and* running a business—are all intensely creative endeavors.

Not an ordinary book on practice issues or finance, *Designing Profits* explains the application of design thinking to business decisions. In fact, that's what makes this book so unique. As a consequence, this will be remarkably accessible—even interesting—to architects, engineers, and construction professionals. ***It is indeed possible to be as creative in establishing and operating a practice as in designing and constructing a building.*** Linking design thinking to operations is a recurring theme in the book.

A successful architectural[1] practice requires principals and staff at every level who are creative, technically proficient, and business-savvy. Or, to think of it conversely, one weak link in the chain can lead to failure. That maxim is particularly applicable to business judgment. One mispriced project is all it may take to wipe out a year's profits or a firm's cash reserves.

*Designing Profits* focuses on that component that is so elusive for so many designers, engineers, and construction professionals—the generic business aspects of practice. It is understandable that design professionals have rarely cultivated an active interest in this area. If anything, it's an ancillary thought; something that's easily assumed will fall into place when good designs are the product of good work performed by good people.

After all, that assumption is implicitly perpetuated by the typical architecture academic curriculum at whose core is, of course, the design studio. The single required professional

---

1   The term "architectural" or "architect" used here and subsequently throughout the book is intended to be representative of various entities in the design and construction industry such as engineers, interior designers, landscape architects, constructors, and other building- and design-related consultants.

practice course in most accredited programs barely scratches the surface. There is thus little training in school and not much available after graduation to prepare professionals for making wise *business* decisions other than perhaps the school of hard knocks, which often turns out to charge the most expensive tuition. It's also a school from which not everyone successfully graduates.

Maintaining the status quo—traditional practice with business as usual—is simply insufficient to survive in today's erratic and demanding economic climate. *Designing Profits* offers comprehensive guidance for design professionals to reap financial rewards from their practices and to discover, precisely analyze, and implement innovative strategies to become entrepreneurial and creative, leading to more opportunities for satisfying design work, a competitive advantage, and just rewards for a job well done.

Discussions about entrepreneurial practice models, smart fees, growth, and—yes—dreaded but essential accounting processes are intended to trigger ideas and inform business decisions. Accounting is viewed in a new light—not as a boring, distasteful, somewhat arcane necessity for complying with tax and payroll requirements, but as a tool for innovative management and a genuine resource for the practice. Ideas underlying accounting data and operational data are fully illuminated and are given new meaning in order to understand and direct both practice and project management.

*Designing Profits* is written primarily for practicing architects, consulting engineers, constructors, and allied specialists in the building industry—such as interior designers and landscape architects—as well those in various building trades. This book is especially timely because of the revolutionary changes occurring in the design and construction industry together with challenging economic cycles. These changes and challenges are viewed as great opportunities to forge new alliances, create specialty niches, optimize work planning, and develop other advanced business tactics.

*Designing Profits* will be equally valuable to seasoned professionals, new graduates, and those in between but not necessarily for the same reasons. Experienced professionals who are dissatisfied with the financial performance of their enterprises will find the principles and solutions described herein to be highly advantageous and immediately applicable to their own circumstance. Recent graduates and emerging professionals, on the other hand, will find not only the basics they need to start their careers on the right foot but also more sophisticated strategies that will be useful as their jobs evolve and they assume increasing responsibilities.

Practitioners constantly whine and complain that students do not learn enough about business in school. And for the most part, they're right.[2] So *Designing Profits* was written with a strong secondary audience in mind as well: students in architecture, engineering,

---

2   This is not to suggest that immersion and time in design studio should be compromised but, rather, in the absence of innovative curricula, conventional professional practice courses should include more material on business-related topics.

construction management, landscape architecture, and interior design. Required professional practice courses across these disciplines are sorely in need of a *focused* resource on business to complement the current handbooks and textbooks that are typically assigned, and that provide a good, general overview of many of the issues of practice. Notwithstanding a radical change in architecture program curricula, reading *Designing Profits* in the context of a conventional professional practice course will address a gap that has existed for too long.

Moreover, for those students, as well as the newly minted graduate in search of employment or, for that matter, anyone who is between jobs, *Designing Profits* offers a way to think about presenting oneself not only as a talented professional but also as one who accretes financial value for an employer. Conveying sensitivity to a prospective employer's financial needs in an interview or an application is sure to be a positive differentiator from the candidate pool, if not a unique one.

Additionally, other professionals who work regularly with design firms will similarly benefit in terms of servicing their design clientele from the insights that *Designing Profits* offers. CPAs, lawyers, insurors, bankers, Realtors®, and contractors, to name a few, may be particularly interested. As a bonus, we predict that many will find—sometimes with a little bit of their own creative thought and sometimes by spontaneous recognition—that more than a small portion of the tools and strategies contained herein can be profitably applied to their own enterprises.

For the two of us authors, this book grew out of our personal friendship and the interest that we each had in the other's profession. Both of us also held faculty positions for which we had shared ideas and observations, which fortuitously sparked the sharing of concepts across professional lines. Plus, both of us had written other books. From there, it was but a short intellectual journey to the idea of authoring a book together.

We were able to write effectively about the intersection of design and business by collaborating. Our co-authorship yielded insights about the two disciplines that would not have been possible otherwise. One author (Andrew), an architect, has deep experience not only in architecture and design but also in educating architects and architectural students across the spectrum of practice types. The other author (Maury), a controller and accountant in both privately held and public companies who turned attorney, has years of experience both as a hands-on financial administrator and as a counselor to his clients on financial and business-related legal issues. This blend of practitioner and advisor is unprecedented in publications in this field.

We would like to underscore that no project is too small to benefit from the powerful tools described in *Designing Profits*. And likewise, no firm is too big to benefit from the insights and strategies presented in the book. We implore you to spend a relatively brief amount of time to become immersed in the ideas—it will be a worthwhile investment in advancing your practice.

A firm must make a profit, do good work, and take care of its staff or else it won't be around for the next project. Consider *Designing Profits* as a fresh toolkit for optimizing time, money, and people in accordance with a firm's mission and vision—*and* personal hopes and dreams.

**Morris A. Nunes**

Waleska, GA

May 2015

**Andrew Pressman, FAIA**

Washington, DC

May 2015

# ACKNOWLEDGMENTS

Francesca Ford, Senior Editor, Architecture—now Publisher, Architecture & Construction—is such a dedicated editor that she reviewed our proposal and provided constructive feedback *when she was on maternity leave*. Just incredible. We are so grateful to have worked with her on this project and hope to work with her on many more.

We owe special thanks to Jennifer Schmidt who covered for Fran and served as Commissioning Editor, shepherding the proposal through various reviews and approvals.

Thanks to William Haggerty, CPA, of Bethesda, Maryland for providing assistance with sample financial statements and chart of accounts. And to Ben Zurich, VP and Controller of KTA Group Inc. of Herndon, Virginia, for providing some insight on professional operations from the financial perspective.

We also wish to thank the entire Routledge production team including Trudy Varcianna, Editorial Assistant – Architecture, Alanna Donaldson, Senior Production Editor, and Maggie Reid, Copy-Editor.

We want to express our sincere appreciation to the three peer reviewers for their thoughtful criticism and support.

I (A. P.) would like to acknowledge Peter Pressman from whom I have learned so much about the art of writing.

And finally, we are grateful to Richard N. Pollack, FAIA, FIIDA, of Pollack Consulting for writing such an eloquent Foreword.

# 1

*Step back from obvious solutions. Instead of trying to invent a better mousetrap, for example, look at other ways to mouseproof your home. Maybe the mousetrap isn't really the problem.*

—Tom Kelley and
David Kelley[1]

*Keep your feet on the ground and keep reaching for the stars.*

—Casey Kasem

# BRIEF OVERVIEW: FORMULATING WISE BUSINESS DECISIONS

The overarching goal of *Designing Profits* is to help architects, and indeed all design professionals, to make wise, objectively based business decisions that lead to maximizing profit and supporting excellent work. Because the art and science of decision-making is a process, the ideas are

1  Tom Kelley and David Kelley, *Creative Confidence: Unleashing the Creative Potential Within Us All*, New York: Crown Business, 2013, p. 101.

often scalable; albeit scalability must be undertaken and leavened with good business judgment. The book aims to provide valuable advice for principals and staff in firms of all sizes, from small to large, and includes tools for refining that very sense of good business judgment.

We would like to underscore that developing good business judgment is a skill that can be learned and finely honed until it becomes second nature. Analogous to drawing, for example, many people believe that innate talent is required. But this is simply not the case with either drawing or business acumen. With sufficient motivation, proper attitude, knowledge, and experience, the business aspects of practice can be learned and even mastered. Our fondest hope is that *Designing Profits* will help you to do just that.

Since every firm has different professional goals and circumstances, there is no single formula for financial success. Therefore, the process that is set forth in *Designing Profits* critically examines the salient issues, provides clear examples, and suggests how the reader's own practice and the economic environment in which it operates might be analyzed and evaluated. Then the material can be applied and customized for best results in support of the distinctly unique needs and goals animating the practice.

## MAKING BUSINESS DECISIONS IS A DESIGN PROBLEM

We would like to introduce a new—and natural—way for design professionals, construction industry stakeholders, and students to think about business: view the process of making business decisions as a unique design problem. The single most important point in *Designing Profits* is that the business process can be as creative and compelling as the firm's design services in order to achieve the firm's goals.

Thinking about all aspects of business in design terms is a way to actively engage with the issues rather than glazing over and becoming comatose with the mere mention of business or its subtopics. But first, an understanding of business basics and tools, as set forth herein, is necessary to inform design thinking and astute decision-making in the business realm.

As with design thinking, the business decision-making process is conceptually straightforward: define the problem; ideate/synthesize/identify alternatives; collect reliable data; calculate costs, benefits, risks, and expected outcomes; refine the implications through testing; and use judgment to finally decide. The process may be iterative, requiring successive loops, each of which produces more information and resolution than the previous one. The resolution may also crystallize or suggest reframing of problems and questions to be addressed.

Similar to design, it's both an art and a science. All the ingredients of a wonderfully challenging design problem are present, from rigorous research and analysis to intuition and epiphany. This approach is in direct contrast to what the decision-making process should not be and so often is—*ad hoc*, arbitrary, and haphazard.

And just as development of an excellent design—an aesthetically pleasing and fully feasible project that fulfills its functional purposes—is a gratifying experience, so too is the development and execution of a well-designed business plan. Plus, there is the tangible reward of the security of a well-cushioned bank account!

What might be an effective way to demonstrate how to apply design thinking to the realities of everyday practice with all the stress, strain, and pressure of deadlines and financial burdens? The next chapter introduces Michelangelo & Brunelleschi Architects LLC, an imaginary, fairly typical example practice that is actually an amalgam of real practices, which is intended to make the material come alive.

We must note that in order to keep our example and its constituent representations relatively transparent and not overly complex, we necessarily had to deal with a smaller enterprise. (We chose that last word purposefully.) Nevertheless, the examples, dilemmas, problems, and particularly the solutions presented are themselves designed in such a way to lend themselves to scaling. That was not such a difficult task as many business issues are universal, many business principles are truly axiomatic, and while organizations do influence how people may respond and relate to one another and their responsibilities and opportunities, people are still people. So whether you are a reader in a larger—even a much larger—enterprise (that economic word again) or a one-person show, you can be assured that you will still find value within these pages.

## THE ARCHETYPAL CASE STUDY

An extended case study is woven throughout the book, chronicling the Practice adventures of the mythical firm Michelangelo & Brunelleschi Architects LLC (M&B). Readers will witness the trials and tribulations as well as the successes of the Principals, Mary Michelangelo and Bob Brunelleschi, in overcoming these challenges, which are, for better or worse, all too common in this field. Readers may readily relate to the scenarios as our heroine and hero encounter issues such as difficult clients, tight project budgets and schedules, marketing challenges, quirky staff, and technology upgrades, just to name a few. Watch them transcend an existential crisis—trying to reconcile the potentially conflicting goals of fostering more meaningful work, larger profit margins, and motivated staff.

The details of the case study will demonstrate the application of objective tools in a practice context. We introduce, as well, M&B's business consultants, Joseph Sloan and Alfred Wharton of Sloan & Wharton Inc. They are a useful author's device, explaining how to properly compile and present, then translate financial and accounting data into the most revealing statements, analyses, and reports—and subsequently suggesting how to interpret and act on the information. M&B's detailed financial statements and comprehensive operating statistics will be analyzed and will serve as a point of departure for understanding financial information and illuminating salient challenges and solutions. Moreover, the profit planning tools discussed herein provide invaluable guidance in conducting what-if scenario testing, which not only allows modeling for decisions but also provides a modality for contingency planning.

We think all of our readers will also be quite at home with the mathematics employed in the examples, none of which are more demanding than introductory algebra. More courageous souls may recognize opportunities for higher mathematics that can be used for more sophisticated modeling, simulating, and testing; but even in such cases, the test always reverts to the simple and basic business formula:

Profit = Revenues – Expenses

Readers should be able to immediately identify with the main players in the case study, from Principals to Interns, as well as the many dilemmas that arise in the course of their practice. Here are some examples of questions—posed as dilemmas—that M&B must wrestle with together with their consultants Sloan and Wharton. Can M&B afford to hire a dedicated marketing person? How should M&B compensate their staff so that it becomes a meaningful incentive to do good work? *How can M&B reduce overhead and increase revenue?* And perhaps most important as the point of analytical departure, how can M&B revise their accounting to quickly get the transparency they need in financial information to make wise decisions on both micro and macro issues?

M&B will need to resolve some additional fundamental questions about the very nature of their practice including whether or not to risk a change in course and, to some extent, business philosophy in order to pursue a more entrepreneurial model; and if so, how this should be approached. Are they interested in expanding the traditional architectural services pie and creating a super-consultancy with unique alliances, or are they more inclined to focus on a niche of specialized services? Once they revisit the Firm's hopes and dreams—the passions of its Principals *and* its staff—can they then align those with the financial picture to arrive at a very customized, bold new direction, one they hope will lead to more profits and professional satisfaction?

Then the whole issue of fees and proposals comes into play with the question of whether fees ought to be solely based on time, on construction cost, or on some other more appropriate (and better) metric. In any case, another question arises: whether any particular project can be properly positioned in the client's mind to yield sufficient profit without sacrificing quality, ensuring also that the design is a worthy one that adds to the Firm's experience and reputation.

If any of those questions are of special and immediate interest, or if you're curious to know what all these dilemmas are, or if you're interested in looking directly at their solutions, a complete listing of the dilemmas with reference to the discussion of the solutions can be found in Chapter 2.

# DECISION CONSEQUENCES

Business decisions and financial constraints impact all aspects of practice, and many business decisions are interrelated—just like design decisions. Another analogy is to view making a business decision as solving a simultaneous equation with many variables, each having different priorities. It is critical to rigorously and objectively integrate the business aspects of practice with the emotional desires for interesting, meaningful work and/or work that will bring recognition. The two realms are not at all mutually exclusive; rather, if viewed strategically, they should be and can be mutually reinforcing. Our objective is to demonstrate this in the book, as summarized in the section that follows and in Figure 1.1.

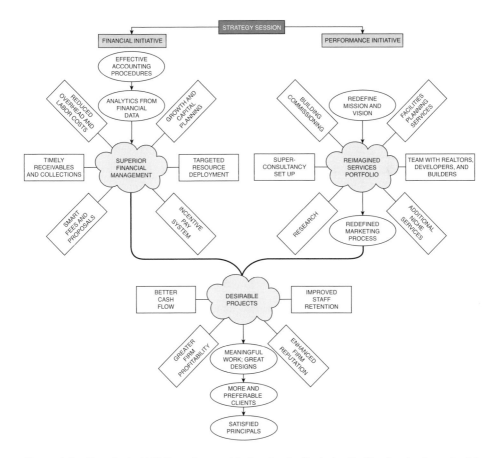

**Figure 1.1**   Coordinated initiatives diagram. Master plan for *Designing Profits*, showing the potential outcomes of new initiatives related to superior financial management and a reimagined services portfolio.

# THE MASTER PLAN

There are two fundamental and simultaneous initiatives described in the book: the *financial initiative* and the *performance initiative*. Each alone has great potential to lead firms to higher profits, meaningful work, enthusiastic staff, great designs, and satisfied clients. In tandem, the two initiatives will have a multiplier effect.

The intention is that initial and ongoing strategy sessions be conducted, either independently or as a component of any strategic planning session, to undertake these initiatives and evaluate the outcomes. The elements of the initiatives are elaborated in detail throughout the book. Refer to Figure 1.1 for a graphic depiction of these two initiatives, described below.

## The Financial Initiative

The first initiative introduced, from which many benefits emanate, objectively focuses on effective accounting procedures that then lead to mathematical analytics derived from hard financial data. Those benefits may reveal the most profitable project types, where to concentrate efforts for timely collections, growth possibilities, how best to reduce overhead and labor expenses, insights into investing resources, and strategies for demonstrating value as evidence for justifying higher fees.

## The Performance Initiative

The second initiative is considered after revisiting the firm's mission and vision, together with the personal hopes and dreams of principals and staff. The focus is on how and what services may be most effectively offered and performed, with options from a super-consultancy to a specialized niche and including those not previously imagined. Those options are not necessarily exclusive and therefore have the potential to yield additional options that might be derived from various hybrids and amalgamations.

Both initiatives are evaluated in a strategy session, referred to above, to see how they might best complement each other and productively align. The alignment naturally leads to a new or redirected marketing effort and business development plan.

So long as the firm's management monitors and adjusts the plan as needed in light of changing conditions and as long as execution and performance are equal to the plan then . . . *voila!*—the final outcome sought above: higher profits, meaningful work, enthusiastic staff, great designs, and satisfied clients.

## Chapter Abstracts

Accounting—tracking the money—is examined in Chapter 3 after the initial description and practice scenarios of M&B Architects are presented in the preceding Chapter 2. Essential information on different types of accounting methods is set forth to develop a basic under-standing of a practice's financial performance. This underpins the ensuing discussion about financial statements—their structure, content, formatting, frequency, and delivery, all of which have a part to play in facilitating decisions to be at least good ones if not, realistically, optimal.

Chapter 4 focuses on analysis, showing how data can be manipulated to control costs and to reveal other relevant information for best management of a practice. Topics include cash flow, receivables analysis and accomplishing their collection, overhead conceptualization and control, development of meaningful metrics, and many others. There is also a noteworthy section that details an innovative method for compensating employees, which is frequently the leading determinant of a firm's ability to reach its goals because of the impact on morale, performance, and client relations.

Growth needs to be understood in all of its multidimensional flavors and perspectives. Chapter 5 tackles this subject head-on with a conversation about revenue growth and analy-sis including the implications of staff efficiency and utilization rates. Some questions that will be answered here include the following: How much additional revenue can be earned with present professional staff, and what is the staff's capacity for taking on more work? What steps would yield more revenue with the current staff? At what point does it make sense to add professional staff? What are the financial ripple effects, especially on overhead and profit margins, if staff is added?

Chapter 6 deals with strategic financial planning issues, which consider both external fac-tors such as the economy and some specific market indices and internal factors such as time—the most precious resource of all. Investing in hiring another member of staff—an Administrator or a Marketing Specialist, for example—will be analyzed using mathematical tools (i.e. Breakeven Analysis or Profit Target Analysis) to facilitate the most profitable decision choice. Steps in managing risk and strategies for financing round out Chapter 6.

With its ideas about rethinking traditional practice, Chapter 7 gets to the heart of the per-formance initiative. A reimagined services portfolio, including investigation of numerous entrepreneurial opportunities and practice models, is the outcome. The sensitive issue of fees is also deliberated here. A substantive discussion of resource investment in support of practice goals completes Chapter 7.

Chapter 8 examines the benefits of staff involvement with clients, administrative tasks, and business development—all integral to a new view of firm culture. Collaboration is a current buzzword for good reason, especially in light of the establishment of super-consultancies, conduct of research, and the option of offering niche services. How to improve the soft skills involved in effective collaboration is briefly reviewed. Ending the book is a salient narrative about gracefully and fairly ending one's involvement in the practice; i.e. how to succeed at succession.

Every reader is, of course, welcome to examine this book in whatever way is desired. However, while it may be tempting to look first at the chapter that is foremost among the reader's concerns or interests, we strongly recommend Chapter 3—pedestrian as mere accounting may seem to some—as the foundation for so much of what follows. Finance is, after all, a scientific art that is dependent on numbers by which success and failure in the form of profit—or their negative, a loss—are measured. But finance is still an art as there is no doubt that the *mélange* of worldly life for all the participants in a practice cannot help but influence the output of those lordly numbers. That's where management comes into play in determining that profit. Rather than profit as a result of management by crisis, or by objective, or by default, or by exception, we suggest that the best management for regularly yielding profits is *management by design*.

*It is essential to view
constraints as a positive
reference for interrogation
and invention rather than as
a limitation.*

—Charles Gwathmey[1]

# MEET THE FIRM: MODEL FOR ANALYSIS

**M**ary Michelangelo
and Bob
Brunelleschi
dragged cushioned
wicker armchairs across
the hot sand to a shaded
area underneath a big
umbrella—the perfect
place to talk while
preserving their gorgeous
view of the turquoise
Caribbean. Mary and Bob
had recently arrived at this

1    Charles Gwathmey, interview by
     Andrew Pressman, New York, NY,
     June 1995.

lush tropical resort for a three-day weekend to reflect on their architectural Firm's history, current challenges, failures, successes, and most importantly, future direction.

After a long sip on his colorful drink, Bob mused: "While I've always been skeptical of the benefits of formal 'retreats,' I realize that if we are to survive and prosper—and break away from our traditional Practice—we must take time to do the clichéd task of taking stock of where we are in addition to the not so clichéd undertaking of *designing* our future in terms of the Practice." The two partners' main objective was to create a roadmap that would lead to achieving professional satisfaction for themselves and their staff as well as relatively large profit margins for the Firm. And so began a couple of days of intense evaluation, diagnosis, analysis, planning, and creative design.

## FIRM HISTORY AND STRUCTURE

Mary took a deep breath and suggested: "Before we begin to plan our future, let's take a step back and review our initial motivations, strengths, and weaknesses—why we launched our Practice in the first place." Bob nodded in agreement as he was flipping through a

**Figure 2.1**   The perfect setting to reflect on a firm's history, current challenges, failures, successes, and most importantly, future direction.

Photo © Andrew Pressman.

folder: "Let's revisit our 'About Us' statement from the Web site, and assess whether our vision is still sound and our plan to achieve that vision still makes sense.

"Here's what I'm looking for; this is what it says on our official Michelangelo & Brunelleschi Architects LLC Firm Web site."

We are passionate about great design. We aspire to:

- Lift the spirit; create magical spaces and places, and beauty and delight on every project;

- Elicit and respond to client, user and other stakeholder requirements and dreams; ensure that a project works efficiently and functionally for its intended use;

- Innovate in order to work with challenging construction budgets;

- Strive for sustainability and always be environmentally sensitive;

- Be contextually responsible; contribute to the surroundings; fit with the region, neighborhood, adjacent buildings, and spaces;

- Incorporate a collaborative process with clients, users, and constructors.

As they began to talk, they couldn't help reminiscing a bit about the good old days of innocent youth when everything seemed possible and future success was inevitable.

Mary and Bob first met in architecture school—a prestigious and rigorous Ivy League 3.5-year graduate program. With complementary skills and abilities, they helped each other excel through the design studios. This successful collaboration, while frowned upon by their professors, foreshadowed their working relationship several years into the future.

During her last semester of graduate school, Mary was aggressively recruited by a large architectural firm with offices in a dozen cities around the world. Her internship and subsequent years in the Boston office provided excellent technical training and opportunities in project management on large commercial and institutional buildings, not to mention some travel to exotic locations in the Middle East. She became an expert in technology and how the pieces fit together and could be expressed artfully in the architecture.

In contrast, Bob chose quite a different path after graduation. His passion was small-scale custom residential projects (see Figures 2.2, 2.3, and 2.4). He loved developing the intricate spatial and spiritual qualities inherent in beautiful house design as well as the profound relationships unique to this client type. Bob was fortunate to have discovered (and have been hired by) a local practice with that specialization, which was highly regarded by architecture colleagues (as evidenced by design awards) as well as the popular press (as evidenced by glossy magazine cover stories). Bob was given design responsibility for everything from small additions and renovations to large new house commissions.

**Figures 2.2–2.4**  Series of images depicting one of Bob's award-winning residential renovation projects that generated publicity and leads for future commissions.

Photos © Chris Spielmann.

Bob and Mary would meet from time to time to catch up and offer advice on their respective work situations and career trajectories. After a few years of the occasional lunch meeting, they both revealed that they were increasingly frustrated with their employers on several dimensions. Mary wanted more control over design, decision-making, and client relations while Bob was tired of huge responsibility with minimal public recognition. They both felt they deserved more money.

The eureka moment happened at lunch, 12 years after graduating, over salads and bacon cheeseburgers. Recalling the magical learning experiences in design studio and their idealistic collaborations, Mary had a crazy idea: "How would you like to do one more big collaboration and start a practice together?" Bob was ready. Their history of working together, comple-mentary skill sets, and shared passion for design excellence suggested they would be great partners. So with years of experience and hundreds of contacts between them, they decided to take the plunge.

At that point in time, Bob had been approached by a prospective client who wanted a 7,500 square foot house on the Maine coast. Bob felt he could bring that project into the new Firm. And Mary was having informal conversations with a developer friend who was thinking about a speculative office building in a Boston suburb. If Mary could close that deal then their new Firm could be up and running with work that could at least pay start-up costs, expenses, and overhead for a few months.

Bob and Mary quickly decided to create a limited liability company and find rental space. The immediate challenge was to select a location that was far enough outside the city that it had affordable office rents yet provided easy access to the city. In addition, they wanted to be in close proximity to several accredited schools of architecture where they both held adjunct faculty appointments. They could not only enjoy teaching part-time but could also tap in to a great pool of emerging talent for the Firm.

## RECENT CLIENTS AND PROJECTS

"C'mon, Mary," Bob said. "We've got to take advantage of this time and *focus*! I'll take some notes so we can at least get the problems down and then we can prioritize them."

Bob opened a new file in the word processing program in his laptop and then hesitated for a moment. Muttering to himself but looking at Mary, he said, "Actually these notes ought to go in a project file in our new scheduling app."

"Wow, Bob!" replied Mary. "You are Mr. Serious today. Go for it!"

Their discussion continued as they considered their present status and began to articulate the challenges facing the Firm. M&B Architects had evolved successfully during the last few years. For a variety of reasons including local economic conditions, personal contacts, and even a bit of serendipity, the Firm's bread and butter work became tenant buildouts, both

**Figure 2.5**  M&B Architects' design for a medical office, representative of the firm's foray into the realm of tenant buildouts.

Photo © Chris Spielmann.

large and small scale (see Figure 2.5). They also have deep experience in custom residential and new suburban office buildings. They have completed a few public buildings including branch libraries and a community center. Their current portfolio is rounded out with a bookstore, a medical office, and a coffee shop. Most of their work is local, but they follow select existing commercial clients out of state when needed. There is some residential work in Florida and the Midwest with a few houses in Europe and the Caribbean as well.

They routinely submit work for national and regional design awards and publications, and they have been somewhat successful in getting recognized for their work.

*Dilemma #1: How can we leverage our seemingly diverse project experience—and staff—for more work opportunities? Can we afford a dedicated marketing person? Can we afford not to have someone take the lead on business development?*

"I'm beginning to think we have problems with client relations," said Mary, "and this is crucial to our business; client relations is so important for referrals, repeat work, and quite frankly, our reputation. I don't think we're getting enough repeat work. I'd like to frame my perception of the problem by first emphasizing two points that fundamentally underlie our engagements with clients: (1) we truly regard the client as a collaborator who can inform and, in some cases, even enrich the design; with the caveat that (2) simply responding to client needs and preferences—at face value—should *never* be an excuse for poor design. Maybe we are a bit too aggressive in pushing our agenda of design excellence on this last point—and sometimes that gets us into trouble with clients. But if we don't do that, why did we become architects in the first place?

"I would add that clients—individuals or building committees—may think they know what they want, but most of them, not having been trained in design, are not able to imagine what is possible architecturally, which is presumably why they hire us! Perhaps we're not as tactful as we should be. After an initial honeymoon period, most of our clients become difficult and require a lot of handholding, which is time-intensive. And I know that we've lost more than a few clients to other firms. Bob, remember that one couple who fired us because they presumably didn't like the colors we selected for their bedroom? It seems as though we are not understanding and not managing client expectations on all dimensions, from fees to design to getting paid."

Bob agreed: "We use the clichéd phrase 'service oriented' on our Web site, which has become synonymous in some circles with pleasing the client at all costs even if it means compromising design. You know that our definition of 'service oriented' means being responsive to the client but also doing something *meaningful* with the project. Perhaps we need to bolster our communication skills—whatever that means."

---

*Dilemma #2: How can we optimize our client relations so we can improve designs and get repeat work and referrals? Could a new business development person assist us with client relations?*

---

## OFFICE SPACE

Mary and Bob were fortunate to find 1,000 square feet of raw space in an old warehouse with great architectural potential that was contiguous to a quaint square in a Boston suburb. First project for Michelangelo & Brunelleschi Architects LLC: create a spectacular design (for very little investment) that would garner design awards and publicity for their new Firm and become a distinguishing three-dimensional calling card.

The office is outfitted with some very basic custom workstations/counters built by one of their carpenter acquaintances. Standard two-drawer files are set beneath the counters around the office. Everyone is located in the big, open space—there are no private offices. There is a centrally located table for meetings, conferences, and collaborative work. The only enclosed/semi-enclosed spaces are for a kitchenette food preparation area and a private meeting room.

The lease term for the office space is up next year. One pressing agenda item for their little retreat is to discuss ideal scenarios for future office space.

> *Dilemma #3: We are outgrowing our current space. Should we renew the lease and create a more efficient space plan; find new space to design, buildout, and generate more publicity; work out of our spare bedrooms, have staff telecommute, and rent a meeting space one day per week; or buy? If we buy, do we go for an office condo or a small freestanding office, or do we buy and build?*

## CURRENT PERSONNEL

Mary is considered the "tough-as-nails bad cop" to Bob's easy-going "good cop." They are unsure if this perception by staff, while certainly not a reflection of reality, translates to good management practice. It seems to work well; although they do have what they feel is a high turnover rate. The lost staffers have most often gone to bigger firms that can afford higher pay and more costly benefits; that seems like it has to be a factor too.

> *Dilemma #4: Why do many of our young staff want to leave after three years just when they can be independent and contribute so much? Maybe we are selecting such outstanding, brilliant people that they wouldn't be happy unless they are on their own . . . or is it something we're doing or not doing? What can we do to retain our staff? How should we compensate our staff so that it becomes a meaningful incentive to do good work? Can we afford to do that?*

## Professional Staff

Mary and Bob each draw a salary of $82,000 and anticipate annual bonuses depending on how well the Firm is doing. Mary has been bringing in projects with larger construction budgets and fees than Bob and feels that she is entitled to—at the very least—larger bonuses.

On the other hand, Bob has somehow ended up handling the bulk of the administrative management tasks, from choosing insurance policies and dealing with their landlord to signing the tax returns. In fact, when Bob looked at his time sheets for the last few months, he found that he was spending a full 50% of his time on non-billable, non-project-related work.

Those hours didn't include the time he spent off-hours taking phone calls, writing emails, and reviewing documents relating to that unavoidable administrivia.

In contrast, time records for Mary reveal that she has booked a mere 25% of her time as non-billable.

Taking all that into account, Bob feels that he is the glue that holds the foundational infrastructure together but that this crucial work of his is underappreciated if not wholly unrecognized, especially by Mary. Conversely, she feels that she is the real revenue engine and that Bob's "obsession" with detail is an excuse for him to stay in his comfort zone inside his office.

> *Dilemma #5: How can we resolve the tension related to the Principals' salary and bonuses?*

There are six full-time professional staff in addition to the two Partners (see Figure 2.6).

Piet Svenson, the Firm's only Associate, is a recently licensed architect and has been with the office for several years since Mary recruited him directly from school. He is bright, worldly, hard-working, technically competent, a good designer, and charming and diplomatic with clients—perhaps his strongest quality—according to Mary. Upon being promoted to associate just after passing the licensing exam, he said: "I am so looking forward to the next 25 years with this Firm! I know I can help us to be considered the greatest architectural practice in New England—and the world!" No ego problems there, and prone to exaggeration, both

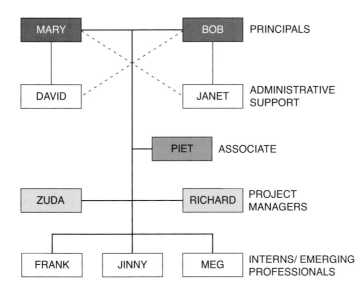

**Figure 2.6**   Current organizational structure of M&B Architects.

Principals agreed. Bob and Mary feel that Piet is the one employee they can readily see as an M&B Partner someday. Salary: $65,000/year with standard benefits (see "Compensation" below).

Zuda Olanju, a Project Manager, has been with the Firm for only a year and a half. She has three years of prior office experience. She is aggressive, likes to wear flamboyant clothing, and has a small tattoo on the back of her neck. She seeks innovation in her work, which is great except when reinventing the wheel takes too much time and eats up profit. She is a good leader and manages the consultants effectively, but she has not yet reached professional maturity. She was given project management responsibility perhaps sooner than she could handle it due to the volume of work in the office, but she rises to the occasion—most of the time. Salary: $56,000/year with standard benefits.

Richard Watson, a Project Manager, is an anomaly. He is in his early sixties yet he never became a registered architect. He has been with M&B Architects for five years after slaving away for much of his professional life at half a dozen large firms in and around Boston—and their Middle East outposts—where he never felt appreciated. He has spent more time on construction sites than everyone else in the Firm combined. His technical expertise makes him invaluable to the Practice. He truly knows how to put a building together—i.e. assemble a set of construction documents—with just the right amount of detail. He is somewhat iconoclastic and arrogant, and he likes to work alone; qualities that tend to alienate him from clients and consultants alike. Thirty-five years ago, he wore a green eyeshade and had many sharpened drafting pencils at the ready in his shirt pocket. Salary: $72,000/year with standard benefits.

Frank Bontano, an Intern who excelled in Bob's design studio at the university, has a lot of confidence, perhaps unwarranted, for his level of experience. He brings the fresh perspective of a smart yet naïve emerging professional; he is therefore valuable at the beginning stages of projects where his design studio experience really kicks in. He doesn't have much technical knowledge but is a quick learner. He has been with the Practice for one year (after a stint lasting a year and a half at another local firm). Salary: $42,000/year with standard benefits.

Jinny Ming is an Intern who has also been with M&B Architects for one year. Mary observed and evaluated Jinny while she was a graduate student in design studios for three years before she joined the Practice. Mary felt that Jinny had great potential as a future Project Manager—and just maybe, eventually, partner—especially after she logs several years of high-quality experience in the M&B office. At design reviews in school, Jinny demonstrated moments of brilliance under extreme pressure from arrogant jurors. She handled belligerent comments with surprising wit and humor while presenting her projects with confidence and intelligence. Her communication skills are one of her obvious strengths. Mary's only reservation was Jinny's inability to consistently work well in a team context. With a little coaching, Mary is sure that she will become a star Project Manager though she is now only a star performer. Salary: $36,000/year with standard benefits.

Meg O'Hara, another Intern, was recruited by Mary right out of architecture graduate school. She provides the Practice with excellent knowledge of software. Typical of her generation, she was brought up on the computer and is facile across platforms and applications. She has made herself the Firm-wide IT resource person. She is hard-working but does not have much practical experience in architecture or construction, other than a couple of summer internships. She has worked at M&B Architects for nine months. Salary: $38,000/year with standard benefits.

Both Frank and Meg have been encouraged to assume increasing responsibility in managing projects.

David Rodriguez, a graduate student, worked this past summer at M&B and is now part-time during the academic year. Salary: $18,000/year, no benefits.

## Nonprofessional Staff

There is only one administrative person. Janet Schwartz serves as an administrative assistant, marketing coordinator, receptionist, office manager, and bookkeeper. She is a nine-to-fiver with family obligations that do not permit her to work overtime. Clearly, she has too many tasks in her portfolio and, therefore, cannot perform any one of them with any degree of thoroughness or excellence. Salary: $36,000/year with standard benefits.

> *Dilemma #6: Should we, and can we, afford to divide Janet's duties and add another staffer?*

## COMPENSATION

Salaries are based on surveys of professional compensation carried out by the American Institute of Architects (AIA) and others, so Bob and Mary believe they are competitive with other similar local firms and pay market rates (see Exhibit 2.1). Their standard benefits are that the Firm pays 50% of the health care insurance premiums and contributes 3% of base compensation to a 401k retirement plan for salaried employees. There is no formal profit-sharing plan but they do have a perfunctory end-of-year evaluation and usually give small pay raises; occasionally they give annual Christmas bonuses. Wine and Cheese Fridays are a chance to socialize and to discuss and critique design, and these are considered a perk.

**EXHIBIT 2.1** M&B Salary Schedule, Year End 20XX

| Employee Name | Position | Annual Pay ($) |
|---|---|---|
| Michelangelo, Mary | Principal | 82,000 |
| Brunelleschi, Bob | Principal | 82,000 |
| Svenson, Piet | Associate | 65,000 |
| Olanju, Zuda | Project Manager | 56,000 |
| Watson, Richard | Project Manager | 72,000 |
| Bontano, Frank | Intern | 42,000 |
| Ming, Jinny | Intern | 36,000 |
| O'Hara, Meg | Intern | 38,000 |
| Rodriguez, David | Part-Time | 18,000 |
| Schwartz, Janet | Administrator | 36,000 |
| **Total Annual Payroll** | | **527,000** |

# PROJECT STRUCTURE

Typically, projects are led by a Principal (either Bob or Mary) who creates the design concepts and is responsible for higher-level client contact. The Principal assigns one of the Project Managers to lead and work with the engineering and other consultants and to translate the design ideas into construction documents. At times, especially with looming deadlines, everyone theoretically will pitch in and work on a project. Job assignments are typically made on a biweekly basis.

During the course of a project—at all phases—both Bob and Mary like to have a hand in the design outcomes through periodically posting and critiquing the work; this sometimes results in time-intensive changes to be implemented (that are sometimes resented) by the staff. In addition, Bob and Mary feel that technical reviews, especially in the latter stages of projects, are very important for design integrity. Occasionally they will ask Richard to conduct this technical review.

*Dilemma #7: Should we offer special training, coaching, or professional development programs to get our staff to collaborate better and manage projects more effectively and efficiently?*

## EQUIPMENT, TECHNOLOGY, AND PROCESS

The Firm's biggest investment lies in computer hardware and software. Currently there are nine workstations—one for each staff member (except part-timer David Rodriguez who logs in as needed on a momentarily vacant workstation) and each of the Principals—connected to their server, which is now beginning to show its age. Most of the construction documents are completed conventionally with 2-D CAD software. They have experimented on a couple of projects with Building Information Modeling (BIM) but have had efficiency problems as well as some resistance from Richard, who complains: "Computer-think is too rigid. No technology fully encompasses how a designer thinks. With all the significant innovations and possibilities envisioned with BIM, there are inherent biases with any modeling tool that may not always support creating the best design."

> *Dilemma #8: We are getting lots of pressure to move into BIM from certain clients who use the deliverables for facilities management. But there is a big learning curve and not all of our consultants are buying into the software—and the Integrated Project Delivery (IPD) process—which would make it optimally effective and efficient. How do we keep up with technology, both in terms of having the right software and equipment and in keeping everyone up to speed on its use?*

All major printing is outsourced. There is one plotter, several color laser printers, a fax machine, a copier, and a telephone system with three outside lines plus one for the fax. A refrigerator, microwave, water cooler, and state-of-the-art cappuccino–espresso machine (perhaps their most important asset) completes the equipment inventory.

## SUCCESSION PLANNING

The underlying philosophy of the Principals of M&B Architects is represented by Woody Allen's famous remark: "I don't want to achieve immortality through my work. I want to achieve it through not dying." Alas, with all the pressure and time constraints of firm start-up—and their relative youth—Mary and Bob simply kept delaying thinking about the future.

Bob insisted that they include succession planning on their retreat agenda or at least discuss how they might initiate the process: "Why don't we be opportunistic about succession planning? If we are smart about it, our plan could be much more than simply a schedule for transferring ownership. It could be integral to our strategic plan to recruit and develop talented staff."

"We can hopefully be compensated fairly for our entrepreneurial efforts when we retire," responded Mary, "but if we look at this as a design problem now, a succession plan has the potential to be much more. I mean, we need to develop and cultivate talented employees in areas beyond design and project management, such as marketing, human resources, financial management, and technology."

> *Dilemma #9: How do we create, and then use and communicate, the succession plan as a tool to hire—and retain—the best people?*

## OTHER CHALLENGES

Mary looked at Bob while shaking her head. "Sometimes I'm baffled when dealing with our employees. Everybody seems to whine constantly about overtime. They want a work/life balance and resent time away from their 'lives.' Oh paleese! Get real! We have deadlines! They say they work smarter not harder. Give me a break. And they say I'm the witch from hell because I sometimes suggest they are lazy and don't get the work done on time. And then they ask for a raise—they are always asking for more money. Not only that, we can't seem to motivate staff to record their billable hours in a timely fashion."

Noticing one of the waiters nearby, Mary waved to him and half-shouted, with an obvious sense of urgency: "Excuse me! Can we get a couple of pina coladas out here on the beach?"

"Yes, indeed. Great idea," Bob smilingly affirmed (referring to the pina coladas). "You're right about some of the staff. Design time always seems to take longer than what we budget for it; maybe our process is flawed because we are so inefficient. But why are we inefficient?"

Bob continued: "We could hire another Intern because we are so busy right now, but there is little backlog in tenant improvement work, which is, of course, one of our primary sources of revenue. Let's consider outsourcing (finding contract employees) instead of adding someone to the Practice. That might give us a bit more flexibility."

> *Dilemma #10: How can we work more efficiently and better control spikes in the work? How do we become more consistent with, and reduce, overtime? How do we get staff to record billable hours and invoice the clients in a timely fashion?*

"And another thing! While I'm disparaging the employees," Mary persisted, "why hasn't anyone updated our Web site from almost three years ago? It's obsolete and, frankly, ugly. Don't get me started on social media. We have an anemic presence at best."

> *Dilemma #11: What are our goals for, and how can we best take advantage of, social media and our Web site?*

"Okay, let's put Web site and social media on the agenda," said Bob, "but I'm not entirely convinced it's all that important for us. What is important, however, is finding a way for clients to pay us on time. Collecting fees has not been one of our strengths and we're suffering because of it."

Dilemma #12: How do we motivate clients to pay us on time?

Bob continued: "Rounding out our list, let's save the most pressing dilemma for last. We certainly want and deserve to make more money, but we also want to work on only the best projects. This is why we went to architecture school in the first place—to do something meaningful and exciting! I know we can easily procure more commissions, but they would involve fairly mindless, repetitive tasks. What's the point of that?"

Dilemma #13: How can we make more profit? How do we reduce overhead and increase revenue? How can we ensure that we have a backlog of interesting design work?

## FINANCING AND CASH FLOW

Bob said: "You know, Mary, as I look at this list of our dilemmas, the depressing thing I keep seeing is the need for more money. I hate to think it's always about the money. We need to figure out how we can afford whatever we decide we want to do. It's prioritizing expenditures and budgeting, but it's more than that; it's projections for cash flow and figuring out how we finance ourselves going forward. Can we safely borrow and how much, and how fast do we pay it back? Do we put more money in, if we can even afford to do that?"

Dilemma #14: How can we finance the necessary improvements to our operations and take advantage of opportunities that present themselves?

## ACCOUNTING AND FINANCIAL INFORMATION

Mary sighed. With a half bitter, half longing look on her face, she said: "Yeah, Bob. The money is always a problem. You remember the problems the last time we went to the bank. They drove us crazy asking for information and we just needed a small amount to finance the new computers and the server. Half the time I didn't understand what they were asking for, and when I did understand, I was lost to figure out how we could get that data out of our system. You know, Bob, I think that, really, we don't have the information we'd need to make smart decisions about a lot of what we've been talking about. Maybe improving our accounting and financial information is where we ought to start?"

Bob pulled up the financial statements file from his hard drive (see Exhibits 2.2 and 2.3) and paged through it for a moment. "I'm looking at the financial statements and they're already months old, and I have no solid idea what's happened since the end of last year."

Bob closed that file and opened another. "The only thing that's up to date is the Salary Schedule" (see Exhibit 2.1). "So we know what people are getting paid. So what? We really don't know how that relates to profits, productivity, capacity, or hardly anything. It seems like the numbers are nothing but overhead, just floating out there until the CPA comes in to do another set of statements at mid-year."

Bob squinted as if looking into the distant future. Then he began nodding his head in agreement. The squint disappeared as he looked straight at Mary and said: "You're right, Mary. We are clueless! This should be our immediate priority."

> Dilemma #15: How do we revise our accounting to quickly get the transparency in financial information we need to make wise decisions on both micro and macro issues?

**EXHIBIT 2.2** M&B Balance Sheet, Year End 20XX

| ASSETS | ($) | LIABILITIES | ($) |
|---|---|---|---|
| Cash in Bank | 22,141 | Accounts Payable | 114,367 |
| Petty Cash | 214 | Accrued Expenses | 44,252 |
| Accounts Receivable | 388,955 | Accrued Taxes | 3,094 |
| Refundable Deposits | 20,000 | Client Deposits | 61,000 |
| Tax Deposits | 22,400 | Loan Payments Due w/in 1 Year | −31,923 |
| Prepaid Assets | 18,840 | Bank Debt: Local Bank | 222,976 |
| Equipment | 104,179 | Financing Lease | 8,836 |
| Furnishings | 38,622 | Shareholder Loan: Michelangelo | 74,000 |
| Vehicles | 84,361 | **TOTAL LIABILITIES** | **496,602** |
| Leasehold Improvements | 129,559 | | |
| Less: Depreciation | −113,520 | **MEMBERS' EQUITY** | |
| Intangibles | 28,450 | Brunelleschi Equity | 115,265 |
| Less: Amortization | −17,070 | Michelangelo Equity | 115,265 |
| | | **TOTAL MEMBER EQUITY** | **230,529** |
| **TOTAL ASSETS** | **727,131** | **TOTAL LIABILITIES & EQUITY** | **727,131** |

**EXHIBIT 2.3** M&B Profit and Loss Statement, Year End 20XX

| REVENUES | $1,546,141 |
|---|---|
| **Expenses** | |
| Advertising & Promotion | 12,029 |
| Automobile Expenses | 9,859 |
| Bad Debts | 14,100 |
| Bank Charges | 2,895 |
| Charitable Contributions | 2,000 |
| Computer Expenses | 17,702 |
| Consultants | 24,000 |
| Depreciation & Amortization | 62,089 |
| Dues | 16,200 |
| Employee Benefits | 65,474 |
| Equipment Lease | 8,836 |
| Insurance | 42,108 |
| Interest | 16,545 |
| Legal & Accounting | 23,942 |
| Licenses | 5,250 |
| Maintenance | 12,880 |
| Meals & Entertainment | 47,154 |
| Miscellaneous Expenses | 19,245 |
| Office Expenses | 16,893 |
| Outside Services | 8,750 |
| Payroll | 527,000 |
| Payroll Taxes | 41,612 |
| Penalties | 1,807 |
| Printing & Reproduction | 12,994 |
| Rent | 50,880 |
| Repairs & Warranties | 11,014 |
| Subcontractors | 294,300 |
| Subscriptions | 18,540 |
| Supplies | 23,303 |
| Taxes | 19,909 |
| Telephone & Fax | 27,516 |
| Training & Seminars | 16,860 |
| Travel | 54,867 |
| Utilities | 11,208 |
| **TOTAL EXPENSES** | **1,539,761** |
| **PRETAX PROFIT** | **6,381** |

**EXHIBIT 2.4** Dilemma Summary, in Order of Importance with Chapter References

| Dilemma | Chapter |
| --- | --- |
| Accounting | 3 |
| Increase revenue | 5, 6, 7 |
| Lower direct costs | 4, 6 |
| Reduce overhead | 6 |
| Collections | 4 |
| Staff retention | 4 |
| Staff increase | 6 |
| Technology | 8 |
| Space | 7 |
| Principals' income | 8 |
| Financing | 3, 6 |

Bob completed his thoughts: "Let's reconsider and revise our agenda items for the retreat in order of importance. Give me a moment to create a new document including a summary list of dilemmas. I'd like to reformat the dilemmas—and combine a few that are interrelated—into general topics, starting with the financials (see Exhibit 2.4). This will further crystallize our perspectives and issues, and it will help us to focus the discussions with our business consultants."

When they seemed to run out of ideas for their brainstorming session to set the agenda for the retreat, Bob and Mary slathered thick layers of sunblock on their now pink and puffy skin and headed for the resort's boathouse for flippers, face masks, and snorkels. There's nothing like floating on the water's surface and looking at tropical fish in preparation for tackling tough business problems. These problems will be addressed as the retreat progresses and, subsequently, as they are presented to the Firm's business consultants, as chronicled in the following chapters.

**3**

## ACCOUNTING: CREATING RELIABLE INPUTS AND OUTPUTS

*The "Information Age."*[1]

*Garbage in; garbage out.*[2]

*As a company gets big, the information that informs decision-making gets massive. Depending upon the prism through which you view the business, your perspective will vary. If two people are in charge, this variance will cause conflict and delay.*

—**Ben Horowitz, Venture Capitalist**[3]

### WHY START HERE?

"Information! We make decisions based on the information we receive and process. So, by the way, does everyone else." Thus spoke Joseph Sloan as his partner, Alfred Wharton, nodded approvingly.

Sloan & Wharton Inc. were the business consultants

1  Unattributed.
2  Unattributed.
3  www.brainyquote.com/quotes/
   authors/b/ben_horowitz.html

Mary and Bob had engaged to help them with their dilemmas. Now back at their office, Mary and Bob—tan, relaxed, and infused with newfound energy—had confirmed to each other their determination to follow through on the output from their retreat.

Wharton chimed in: "When it comes to business decisions, it is hard to imagine an ability to make wise decisions without including accounting data. Accounting, after all, is the language of business." He continued: "Our discussion of business processes and business management begins here with the seemingly mundane process of accounting—including in particular the reporting of accounting results—because the business management of those business processes means making and implementing and monitoring the outcomes of decisions, which cannot be wise or optimal if based on misapprehension, speculation or mere tradition."

Shifting his gaze back and forth between Bob and Mary, Sloan added: "The accounting function is often viewed by non-accountants—and even by some accountants themselves—as a necessary evil, a distasteful overhead function, a joyless task mandated to satisfy the tax authorities in extracting their pound of flesh. Too often, that negative concept yields a self-fulfilling prophecy in which the broad potentialities of accounting to inform and guide wise business decisions are missed.

"Properly perceived and exploited, accounting is quite the contrary. It can be the catalyst that turns apparent dross into gold. It has the potential to be both microscope to ferret out the cause of various maladies, great and small, that may infect the body corporate while also simultaneously being the telescope that can chart a visionary future pathway to the financial stars."

**Figure 3.1**　Accounting does not have to be confusing; if properly perceived and exploited, it can be the catalyst for solving the financial puzzle.

# THE LANGUAGE OF BUSINESS

Alfred had more to say: "Yes, accounting is the language of business. But what is often mis-understood is that, similar to most languages, it has more than one dialect. In each of those dialects, one word may have very different meanings or nuances of meanings that change the import—and often the importance—of what's being communicated by that very word.

"There is a story from World War II about a meeting in which the top American and British strategists were beginning to plan the D-Day invasion. The British suggested that the key question of the number and availability of landing craft to carry the invasion troops ashore on the Normandy coast should be 'tabled.' The Americans were inflamed by this notion that consideration of such a critical question should be delayed and argued vociferously that it could not be tabled. The British argued, amazed at the blindness of these stubborn Yanks, that it must be tabled forthwith. It took some back and forth before the dialectical difference was recognized, and it was understood that both groups wanted to consider the landing craft issue right away. Unlike the Americans, who viewed the verb 'to table' as derived from laying on the table, meaning to set aside, the British dialect viewed this verb as derived from putting on the table, meaning to consider now."

# ACCOUNTING'S EIGHT DIALECTS

We can pick up and build on that theme. The wise practice manager will consider a term like *profit* from more than one perspective, thinking about the different dialects that the language of accounting contains not to mention the fact that accounting often has multiple uses for, and variants of, the same word. *Profit* is particularly such a word.

How many dialects are there? We posit there are *eight* principle dialects with many sub-dialects that vary by field. Here's a brief description of those eight dialects of accounting:

1. **Book Accounting.** This dialect is the one that is commonly thought of when the word *accounting* is mentioned. It is the standard compilation of data in various journals and ledgers (the "books") of the firm, tracking the transactions of the practice. It is defined by *Generally Accepted Accounting Principles* (usually acronymed to GAAP), which are frequently followed for privately held businesses, but not all that scrupulously. (Punsters insist these businesses just follow GAAP *generally*.) The standard penultimate achieve-ment of those speaking only this dialect is to produce a set of typical financial statements, consisting of a *profit and loss statement* (sometimes called an *income statement*) and a *balance sheet*. For purposes of an overview, that is an important achievement whose value should not be minimized; but it alone is not enough. Not at all.

2. **Cash Flow Accounting.** While information feeds the brain of the body corporate, the lifeblood is cash flow. The brain will cease to function if cash dries up. Book Accounting may also be used to calculate a *cash flow statement* (sometimes called a *sources and*

*uses statement*) that shows, again from an overview perspective, how cash has, on balance for any period, been incremented or decremented in the business. Cash flow accounting, however, while including such gross calculations, goes deeper to penetrate and monitor where, when, and why cash is coming in and going out, not only to discern how to increase the in part and minimize the out part but also to assure that sufficient cash is on hand to fund operations and seize opportunities—but not too much as keeping cash has with it an associated cost of capital.

3. **Operational Accounting.** The above two dialects, as indicated, tend to focus on gross results while Operational Accounting looks at the constituent parts of the body corporate. It seeks to isolate the cause and effect relationships of each aspect of operations in order to promote nourishment or pruning as indicated thereby.

4. **Budgetary Accounting.** Formal budgets are rare in smaller practices though informal budgets may be created from time to time on the back of an envelope or may swirl around in the minds of its principals. As organizations grow, the positive tendency exists to create some kind of budgetary system, which is, in essence, both a disciplinary constraint and a futuristic projection. Budgetary Accounting considers those two implicit attributes to determine if and why there are violators of the constraint and to examine the validity of the projections. The most sophisticated speakers of this dialect will also use Budgetary Accounting to monitor the dynamic state of the body corporate and to reposition it and its constituent parts in order to optimize its performance.

5. **Stochastic Accounting.** All four of the preceding accounting dialects deal strictly in the *lingua franca* of money. Stochastic Accounting, while surely including money, goes beyond that bare metric to understand how other metrics relate to money. Professional hours, facilities square footage, number of support personnel, and site visits are just a few examples of the statistics that may be gathered and manipulated to yield management insight toward efficiencies and profitability.

6. **Tax Accounting.** Tax laws, which seem ever-changing and ever more demanding, are an unavoidable consideration for all modern economic undertakings. Income taxes usually command the greatest amount of consideration, but as the search for government revenues continues at many levels, other taxes are affected too. Tax Accounting seeks to lawfully comply with the calculations mandated for tax determination in the most favorable (meaning least tax) manner. Mastery of the applicable dictated rules for doing so is the central precept of that effort.

7. **Regulatory Accounting.** The sister of Tax Accounting, Regulatory Accounting is similarly rule-bound to accurately produce reports required by regulatory authorities. Practices that perform work for governmental entities typically have this kind of reporting duty and thus need to perform compliant Regulatory Accounting. Those practices that do not engage in such work rarely encounter the need for this additional effort. *(It is important to note here, as an aside, that Tax Accounting and Regulatory Accounting share the sometimes*

*unfortunate quality of including theoretical or even arbitrary methods for memorializing transactions. Practices that keep their books and prepare their reports to conveniently comply with either of these two dialects, but ignore the others, are at great risk of being misled by the often artificial nature of such accounting.)*

8. **Management Accounting.** All of the preceding forms of accounting have specific roles to play and more or less predefined realms in which they operate and thus rather predictable boundaries on their utility, most if not all of which is tactical or occasionally grand tactical in scope. Management Accounting, in contrast, is the tool from which managers seek input to make strategic decisions; those decisions that tend to define the fundamental course of the enterprise, at least for the short and intermediate term, if not far longer. The only limits on Management Accounting are those that arise from the questions. Management Accounting thus seeks to synthesize information from all of the other forms of accounting to yield a holistic knowledge of the firm that can translate the present into the optimal future.

The accounting activity consists, at base, of collecting, recording, characterizing, and presenting information about the firm. In all dialects, except Budgetary Accounting and Management Accounting, that information is backward-looking, providing a historical perspective of one kind or another. Budgetary Accounting does not look far into the future and its manner of looking is effectively limited to the framework of the recent past. Management Accounting may and hopefully will include a much greater degree of a look forward into the future, perhaps even the deep future . . .

## REPORTING IS THE KEY

Purists among readers of the above are no doubt shuddering and wondering if this recital means that we need to keep eight sets of books? ABSOLUTELY NOT! We need and should have one and only one set of books, but one that in reality is a database of transactions so that for each type of accounting, we can extract and classify and manipulate and develop the information that managers need to manage.

A set of books (now almost always embodied in a computer program and its constituent parts and storage) is fundamentally a record of money in and money out, characterized packet by packet as an increment or decrement to some kind of revenue, expense, asset, liability or equity, but in double entry fashion so as to maintain a balance among money in, money retained, money owed and money out. Summing the positives and negatives, characterization by characterization, yields the total activity in this or that account for the accounting time period.

Those individual transactions constitute that singular database. In the ideal situation, that database further provides direct links from the recorded transaction to the source documents, like invoices, time sheets, bank deposits, and the like. These source documents are the ultimate micro-view, amplifying and explaining the nature of each transaction so that a manager can understand the accounting characterization (or rationally challenge it), what happened, and most importantly, what lessons might be learned for the future, whether those lessons are based on individual transactions or a collected set, and whether from the evidences of success or the entrails of failure.

In terms, then, of data collection and recordation, there is and should be just that one set of accounting records. Where these accounting dialects diverge for their critical purposes is in the characterization and presentation of the results; i.e. in the *reporting*, which constitutes the culmination of the accounting function.

## ACCOUNTING METHODS

Before we can explore the difference in dialects more deeply, we must divert for a moment to consider the different types of accounting methods. There are three principal methods that logically may be chosen for architects and engineers. Where they differ is the point in time at which certain transactions are recognized, literally meaning "recorded in the books":

1. **Cash Method.** Transactions are recognized (with some few exceptions) only when cash comes into the enterprise (e.g. payment is received from a client) or goes out (e.g. rent is paid).

2. **Accrual Method.** Transactions are recognized at the point in time when legal rights (e.g. the client is billed for work completed) and obligations attach (e.g. rent becomes due in the new month) and those transactions are recorded according to those rights and obligations.

3. **Percentage Completion.** Revenue is recognized project by project according to the portion of the project completed, ratably with direct costs. While Percentage Completion might be married with the Cash Method for costs other than direct, it is most commonly utilized with the Accrual Method for those other costs.

A quick example to illustrate the differences: Assume that on the accounting period's last day, a client is sent a $20,000 invoice in a $100,000 project with $40,000 already billed to and paid by the client. Assume too that the direct costs to complete the project are forecast at $60,000 and only $30,000 has so far been spent, but $5,000 of those charges that have been billed to the firm are not yet paid.

Which of these financial statements would you prefer to present to your banker? How about to the income tax authorities? See Exhibit 3.1.

Important to recognize, however, is that at the end of the project when all the revenues are collected and all the expenses are paid, all three methods will yield the same result in recorded profit. All the different accounting methods are really doing is reflecting timing differences! Yet, those timing differences are transiently critical, potentially making a big difference in what the status and performance of the firm looks like at any snapshot moment when a report or financial statement or tax return is issued.

**EXHIBIT 3.1** Example Illustrating Different Accounting Methods

The three income statements on this project look quite different.

| | $ | Comments |
|---|---|---|
| *Cash Method* | | |
| Revenue | 40,000 | Only this much cash has been received on the Project. |
| Direct Costs | −25,000 | Only this much cash has been paid out for the Project. |
| Gross Profit | 15,000 | |
| *Accrual Method* | | |
| Revenue | 60,000 | But this much has been billed for the Project. |
| Direct Costs | −30,000 | And this much has been legally obligated in total. |
| Gross Profit | 30,000 | |
| *Percentage Completion* | | |
| Revenue | 50,000 | As only ½ the work is done, only ½ the revenue is recognized.* |
| Direct Costs | −30,000 | We know it's ½ the work because it's ½ the projected cost.** |
| Gross Profit | 20,000 | |

Notes: * The other $10,000 is recorded as a liability because if the work is not done, the money is theoretically subject to refund. When the work is done and billed, the $10,000 will be moved out of liabilities and become revenue; i.e. its characterization will be changed.

** You may be asking what happens when the Project ends up with costs different from forecast, as is almost always the case? Then, the true costs and true revenues are recognized for what they are. The point of Percentage Completion is to avoid distortions in the picture of the Firm's performance that can arise strictly because of timing differences in billings and payments. You've probably guessed that this method is not very useful if projects are relatively short in duration or, if longer, fairly uniform in profile. Hence, most firms focus on cash and/or accrual.

*Question:* Which accounting method is best for you?

*Answer:* You need to be able to track cash and know where it's coming from and where it's going, but you cannot be blinded at the arbitrary moment of reporting by cash performance or cash status. You need to be aware of all the differences to understand *why* the results are different and what they each may portend.

## TERMINOLOGICAL IMPLICATIONS

So, how do these eight dialects affect management? Let's consider those words *profit* and *loss* in the context of each of the dialects in order to highlight some of the differences among them.

- **Book.** Profit is the accretion (loss is the decrement) to net asset value (i.e. total assets less total liabilities) arising during the accounting period in which accretion belongs to the owners at the end of that accounting period.

- **Cash Flow.** Profit refers to the increase in cash from operations during the period, while loss is the decrease. Cash can change, however, from nonoperational causes, such as an infusion of equity, payoff of a loan, etc. (N.B. *Surplus* and *deficit* are terms usually used in this context to reflect the overall change in cash from the prior reporting period.)

- **Operational.** Only the net benefit (accrual or cash) from ongoing operations are considered, so extraordinary gains and losses are not considered.

- **Budgetary.** Profits and losses are considered and compared against the backdrop of what was budgeted. Profits may be robust yet disappointing if below budget. The variances from budget are often equally or more instructive than the net result.

- **Stochastic.** Profit or loss here is reported and interpreted in terms of relationships or ratios to statistical inputs and outputs—hours, number of accounts, number of transactions, and other metrics that reflect the underlying fundaments of the monetary transactions. Profits and losses are viewed in terms of efficiencies and discrepancies, hopefully revealing fertile areas for improvement and hidden opportunities.

- **Tax.** Profits and losses are defined here in the format dictated by tax laws and regulations that govern accounting. While there is a strong correlation to a firm's "regular" accounting, knowledge and consideration of the tax accounting implications and their concomitant tax benefit or cost is another factor that the prudent manager will inculcate in decisions.

- **Regulatory.** Similarly, where regulations govern the firm's accounting (e.g. when performing government work), profit and loss will be set in compliance with applicable regulations. If such accounting may impact the firm's welfare by virtue of its recognition of profit and loss (e.g. if government has the right to impose penalties, award bonuses, recover payments, cancel or refigure invoices, or otherwise penalize or reward firms based on accounting reports), the prudent manager involved in such scenarios also has to consider the impact of those regulations when making management decisions and plans.

- **Management.** Profit and loss in this dialect has whatever meaning management wishes to ascribe, as Management Accounting is really about putting together those reports that present true relevant facts upon which wise (preferably optimal) decisions may be accurately based. In that respect, all of the data that the firm collects and that is available to it, including standard data from and about the profession, should be considered as—and ideally is configured as and managed as—a vast database from which such facts can be readily and rapidly called forth, manipulated, presented, and properly understood.

Very much the point of that little differentiation exercise is to alert the manager that the context in which accounting terms are used (i.e. the reporting dialect spoken at any particular time) must be accurately recognized and clearly understood. If the wrong dialect is perceived, the meaning of the report and its contents may be misunderstood or misinterpreted with corresponding decisional deficiencies and action mistakes.

A corollary for the practice manager is to participate in and understand the decisions about the basic choices being made for the firm's accounting system. Those choices include the following:

- What accounting method will be used for financial statements?

- How will a method be reconciled and understood if another method is chosen?

- What accounting software will be used? What choices does it inherently make? What limitations does it have?

- What reports will be issued and with what frequency?

- What burdens and choices are imposed by tax regulations?

- If applicable, what burdens and choices are imposed by other regulations impacting the firm?

Throughout *Designing Profits*, we will be discussing accounting data and what it might tell the manager if properly compiled and presented.

## A WORD ABOUT INTERNAL CONTROLS

Embezzlement and internal fraud are the dirty little secrets of some businesses. While such losses are often uncovered, they frequently are kept confidential for a variety of reasons, ranging from making deals for restitution to fear of undermining client confidence.

Generally speaking—and this may seem counterintuitive—the *smaller* the firm, the greater the risk. And the risks have been multiplying with the advent of electronic banking, computerized books, and remote access, among other technologies. That is not to say that common and hoary dishonest practices such as false vendors, forgery, and in-kind theft are declining.

There are two commonly cited preventatives. One is the careful development and inclusion of system safeguards (e.g. passwords, automatic logs, etc.). The other is creation of overlapping duties so that personnel are inherently overseeing each other. Since most fraud and embezzlement is carried out by individuals acting alone, requiring two signatures or some other form of interaction reduces the risk since the majority of employees will act honestly and the need to engage an accomplice is a practical deterrent in itself.

The more delegation of financial responsibilities and authorities is pushed to lower levels in, and dispersed throughout, an organization, the greater the risks and the greater the needs for these two preventatives. Moreover as the sophistication and complexity of systems grow, the sophistication and comprehensiveness of preventatives has to be updated to match.

The single greatest protection, however, is direct managerial oversight and review of financial data and its reconciliations. Random testing of that data and internal publicity about that practice—not to mention transparency of the books—is in itself a deterrent. This point is one more reason why basic understanding of the accounting system and accounting practices is essential for all firm management.

This brief section is focused on internal risks, but external risks, from hacking to swindles, deserve equal weight in system development and reporting contexts. It is just a fact that businesses are more and more at risk for internal wrongdoing.

## THE NEED TO TRANSLATE DATA

Joseph Sloan and Alfred Wharton listened attentively as Mary and Bob explained that they have historically looked at accounting as a somewhat aggravating overhead expense. They admit that Bob told their CPA that they wanted a minimum of money spent and the CPA accordingly recommended that they use a standard accounting software pack that would keep their books in conformity with the Tax Code; so all the CPA would need to do is simply pull those numbers off at year end, making very few adjustments to complete the tax returns. He would not provide any separate financial statements as M&B can use the tax return, which is what the Firm's bank has asked for each year anyway in order to keep their line of credit active.

While some costs are being saved, the owners are troubled that cash always seems to run short near month's end. Moreover, they have a difficult time developing fee proposals that work out closely to intended results; though now and then some prove to be pleasant surprises.

Mary and Bob have also held back on marketing expenses because they feel they can't be sure that making such expenditures will prove beneficial and don't have a clue about how to analyze that question. They content themselves with the belief that their personal relationships are and remain the best way to generate new business. Of course, they can each only do so much networking and business development because they are so busy turning out work of their own, no small portion of which is necessarily administrative—especially for Bob. Dealing, then, with accounting and financial questions is resented by each as another time suck, and this has always ended up as a low priority.

After listening to this sad tale, Wharton said: "The inability to evaluate the potential benefit or disadvantage of various marketing expenditures is symptomatic of the greater inability to *exploit* the wealth of data that lurks within your Firm's financial history. There are a number of relatively simple and inexpensive steps that can be taken to mine, smelt, and refine some of that data into practice gold."

One step he recommends is to reformat the financial statements. The reformatted financials can offer both an insightful understanding of the past and a genuine glimpse into the future, as explained in the following sections.

## FINANCIAL STATEMENT FORMATTING: THE WHAT

When they examine their financial statements now, Sloan and Wharton explained, all Mary and Bob see is a simple, isolated point in time and an ill-defined one at that. What's ill-defined about it? If we look again at the profit and loss statement in Chapter 2 (Exhibit 2.3), there are a bunch of things we *don't* see:

1. We don't see a breakdown of the *kinds* of revenue among residential, commercial, and government work but, rather, just a single number.

2. We don't see a distinction made among *variable costs* (that correlate directly with revenues, such as the time of the professionals) and *fixed costs* (that generally do not vary with revenues, such as rent) often referred to as *overhead*.[4] Yes, in the very long run, all costs do vary but not in a way that correlates practically in time with revenues.

3. We don't see any matching of *kinds* of revenues with the *costs* necessary to earn those revenues.

4. We don't see any recognition of the profit contribution (or loss) produced from each kind of revenue; i.e. we can't tell if these separate activities are *Profit Centers*.

5. We don't see any sort of relationship identified between costs and the revenues that are essential to cover those costs so that we can focus on the revenues that need to be increased and the costs that need to be reduced.

6. We don't see any comparison to any prior period.

7. We don't see anything that might help us discern trends.

8. We don't see anything that might help us forecast.

In point of fact, there's more than one format that we'll need to use to let us see all of the above—and maybe even more.

## FINANCIAL STATEMENT FORMATTING: THE WHY

As one of those formats, Sloan and Wharton first offer revenue division (Exhibit 3.2), which answers the missing 1 through 5 of *the what* as a lead-in to answering *the why*.

Mary and Bob are both shocked to see that the government work yields so little gross profit: just 12.77%. So small in fact that if they allocate a fair share of the overhead to the government work then M&B is losing money on that work. Wharton agreed that might be true; but

---

4  Accountants also refer to the concept of *semi-variable costs* (that vary as certain thresholds of revenue are passed, such as the need to furnish another workstation once work reaches a certain volume), which are best dealt with by division into their variable and fixed components. We'll deal with semi-variable costs in some detail in Chapter 5.

**EXHIBIT 3.2** Profit & Loss Statement: Revenue Division

| | Residential | Commercial | Government | Total | Revenue (%) |
|---|---|---|---|---|---|
| **Revenue ($)** | **638,324** | **719,381** | **188,436** | **1,546,141** | **100.00** |
| Revenue (%) | 41.28 | 46.53 | 12.19 | 100.00 | |
| | | | | | |
| *Variable Costs* | | | | | |
| Payroll ($) | 224,591 | 147,520 | 57,389 | 429,500 | 27.78 |
| Payroll Taxes ($) | 17,743 | 11,654 | 4,534 | 33,931 | 2.19 |
| Employee Benefits ($) | 27,903 | 18,328 | 7,130 | 53,361 | 3.45 |
| Subcontractors ($) | 108,155 | 104,835 | 81,310 | 294,300 | 19.03 |
| Print & Reproduction ($) | 3,093 | 4,210 | 5,691 | 12,994 | 0.84 |
| Unreimbursed Travel ($) | 4,045 | 10,496 | 8,326 | 22,867 | 1.48 |
| **Total Variable Costs ($)** | **385,530** | **297,043** | **164,380** | **846,952** | 54.78 |
| *Variable Costs (%)* | 60.40 | 41.29 | 87.23 | 54.78 | |
| | | | | | |
| **Gross Profit ($)** | **252,794** | **422,338** | **24,056** | **699,189** | **45.22** |
| Gross Profit (%) | 39.60 | 58.71 | 12.77 | 45.22 | |
| | | | | | |
| *Overhead* | | | | | |
| Advertising & Promotion ($) | | | | 12,029 | 0.78 |
| Automobile Expense ($) | | | | 9,859 | 0.64 |
| Bad Debts ($) | | | | 34,100 | 2.21 |
| Bank Charges ($) | | | | 2,895 | 0.19 |
| Charitable Contributions ($) | | | | 2,000 | 0.13 |
| Computer Expenses ($) | | | | 17,702 | 1.14 |
| Consultants ($) | | | | 24,000 | 1.55 |
| Depreciation & Amortization ($) | | | | 62,089 | 4.02 |
| Dues ($) | | | | 16,200 | 1.05 |
| Employee Benefits ($) | | | | 12,113 | 0.78 |
| Equipment Lease ($) | | | | 8,836 | 0.57 |
| Insurance ($) | | | | 42,108 | 2.72 |
| Interest ($) | | | | 16,545 | 1.07 |
| Legal & Accounting ($) | | | | 23,942 | 1.55 |
| Licenses ($) | | | | 5,250 | 0.34 |
| Maintenance ($) | | | | 12,880 | 0.83 |
| Meals & Entertainment ($) | | | | 47,154 | 3.05 |

| | Residential | Commercial | Government | Total | Revenue (%) |
|---|---|---|---|---|---|
| Miscellaneous Expense ($) | | | | 19,245 | 1.24 |
| Office Expense ($) | | | | 16,893 | 1.09 |
| Outside Services ($) | | | | 8,750 | 0.57 |
| Payroll ($) | | | | 97,500 | 6.31 |
| Payroll Taxes ($) | | | | 7,681 | 0.50 |
| Penalties ($) | | | | 1,807 | 0.12 |
| Rent ($) | | | | 50,880 | 3.29 |
| Repairs & Warranties ($) | | | | 11,014 | 0.71 |
| Subscriptions ($) | | | | 18,540 | 1.20 |
| Supplies ($) | | | | 23,303 | 1.51 |
| Taxes ($) | | | | 19,909 | 1.29 |
| Telephone & Fax ($) | | | | 27,516 | 1.78 |
| Training & Seminars ($) | | | | 16,860 | 1.09 |
| Overhead Travel ($) | | | | 32,000 | 2.07 |
| Utilities ($) | | | | 11,208 | 0.72 |
| **Total Overhead ($)** | | | | **712,808** | **46.10** |
| **Net Pretax Profits ($)** | | | | **−13,620** | **−0.88** |

he said: "Here's the rub if we make an *artificial* allocation: Let's say we do that by applying that business line's revenue percentage—12.19%—to all the overhead items. Then we may rapidly conclude that such work is hurting the bottom line and decide it should be terminated as a loser. Then that 12.77% gross profit contribution will have to be absorbed by residential and commercial revenues, further depressing Company-wide profits if terminating the activity does not actually yield the reduction in overhead at least equal to the allocated overhead.

"That's why all those overhead numbers show up only in the last column dealing with total revenues. If those figures can be analyzed to accurately work out how the overhead figures will *regularly and realistically* vary—if at all—with revenue in each category then it should be allocated accordingly; but for M&B that's not the case because there's not adequate data—at least as of now. In all likelihood, if government activity is terminated then the decline in overhead will be negligible.

"This government activity overhead allocation question *could* be a subject for further study, but the better use of scarce analytical and management resources is more likely to be figuring out *why* government activity is so anemically profitable. Is fee development flawed? Are costs underestimated? Are project managers not performing well? Is that just the nature of government contracting for architectural services?"

**EXHIBIT 3.3** Line Item Percentages

| Variable Costs | Residential (%) | Commercial (%) | Government (%) | Total (%) |
|---|---|---|---|---|
| | 41.28 | 46.53 | 12.19 | 100.00 |
| Payroll & P/R Overhead | 52.29 | 34.35 | 13.36 | 100.00 |
| Subcontractors | 36.75 | 35.62 | 27.63 | 100.00 |
| Print & Reproduction | 23.80 | 32.40 | 43.80 | 100.00 |
| Unreimbursed Travel | 17.69 | 45.90 | 36.41 | 100.00 |
| **Total Variable Costs** | **45.52** | **35.07** | **19.41** | **100.00** |
| Gross Profit | 36.16 | 60.40 | 3.44 | 100.00 |

Analyzing again, Sloan suggested that one tiny clue may lie in the relatively small line item Print & Reproduction, where the least revenue is costing the most. This line item suggests there are more corrections being made with concomitant time being spent. They explode those numbers out some more by calculating how much of each line item is attributable to the line of business (Exhibit 3.3).

From these percentages, they deduce that the real killer seems to be the subcontractors. The payroll factors are compressed into one line item as Payroll Taxes and Employee Benefits are a percentage of Payroll; and they are not that far out of line with the line of business revenue percentage. However, subcontractors, the biggest single cost for government work, is way out of line.

Bob and Mary want to investigate this and see if the problem can be fixed. They might think that if they are going to pursue this work then they need to add a billable staffer who is experienced in dealing with government contracts, which also means that more effort to build up revenues there will be necessary. The strategic implications begin to unfold!

Back to the overall reformatting, note that a couple of line items have been divided between direct costs and overhead: Payroll, Payroll Taxes, Employee Benefits, and Travel, the last of which has been divided into Unreimbursed Travel and Overhead Travel. These allocations are *not* artificial:

- As per the preceding Chapter 2, Jan Schwartz is the sole Administrator and her entire $36,000 salary is overhead.

- And Chapter 2 indicated that Bob spends 50% of his time on non-billable work while Mary similarly spends 25% of her time (i.e. 50% of $82,000 and 25% of $82,000).

- The Payroll Taxes and Employee Benefits are calculated as a straight percentage of Payroll.[5]

---

5   Because Payroll Taxes and Employee Benefits are usually capped and/or tiered, the actual calculation is usually more refined; it is simplified here for illustration, though actual figures would likely not make a material difference.

- Travel is assumed divided based on actual invoices and other travel records.

Some other overview observations that Sloan and Wharton highlight from this portion of reformatting include the following:

- Commercial projects tend to be the most profitable, suggesting perhaps that's where marketing dollars and effort should be focused.

- No overhead number seems all that material, yet in the aggregate they are putting the Company into a loss position, suggesting that some wise tightening up and a search for incremental efficiencies might make the business profitable.

- The average gross profit is not too far from 50% so *if* the overhead can be held at this level, and *if* this gross profit level can be marginally improved, every dollar of added revenue will bring almost 50 cents to the bottom line. That begs the question of capacities as a potential constraint on marketing successes, which necessarily implicates the question of capital needed to fund any successive capacity constraints generated from marketing increases. Much more about this strategic point in Chapter 6.

But wait—THERE'S MORE! Let's look at the reformatted balance sheet (Exhibit 3.4).

**EXHIBIT 3.4** Reformatted Balance Sheet, Year End 20XX

| ASSETS | ($) | LIABILITIES | ($) |
|---|---|---|---|
| *Current Assets* | | *Current Liabilities* | |
| Cash in Bank: Checking | 19,141 | *Payables & Accruals* | |
| Cash in Bank: Savings | 3,000 | Accounts Payable | 114,367 |
| Petty Cash | 214 | Accrued Expenses | 44,252 |
| *Total Cash* | *22,355* | Accrued Taxes | 3,094 |
| Accounts Receivable | 396,893 | *Total Payables & Accruals* | 161,713 |
| Less: Bad Debts Allowance | −7,938 | | |
| *Net Accounts Receivable* | *388,955* | Customer Deposits | 61,000 |
| *Other Current Assets* | | | |
| Refundable Deposits | 20,000 | Loan Payments Due w/in 1 Year | 55,569 |
| Tax Deposits | 22,400 | *Total Current Liabilities* | *278,282* |
| Prepaid Assets | 18,840 | | |
| *Total Other Current Assets* | 61,240 | *Long-Term Bank Debt* | |
| *Total Current Assets* | 472,550 | Bank Debt Eqpt/Furn. Loan | 90,000 |
| | | Bank Debt Term Loan | 77,407 |
| *Intangibles* | | *Total Long-Term Bank Debt* | *167,407* |
| Copyrights | 28,450 | | |
| Less: Amortization | −17,070 | *Other Long-Term Debt* | |
| Net Intangibles | 11,380 | Financing Lease | 8,836 |

**EXHIBIT 3.4** *continued*

| ASSETS | ($) | LIABILITIES | ($) |
|---|---|---|---|
| | | Member Loan: Michelangelo | 74,000 |
| *Fixed Assets* | | *Total Other Long-Term Debt* | 82,836 |
| Equipment | 104,179 | *Total Long-Term Debt* | 250,243 |
| Less: Depreciation | −62,507 | **TOTAL LIABILITIES** | **528,525** |
| *Net Equipment* | 41,672 | | |
| | | **MEMBERS EQUITY** | |
| Furnishings | 38,622 | *Brunelleschi Equity* | |
| Less: Depreciation | −7,724 | Opening Capital Account | 130,113 |
| *Net Furnishings* | 30,898 | Net Income | −6,810 |
| | | Draws | −24,000 |
| Vehicles | 84,361 | YE Brunelleschi Equity | 99,303 |
| Less: Depreciation | −27,839 | | |
| *Net Vehicles* | 56,522 | *Michelangelo Equity* | |
| | | Opening Capital Account | 130,113 |
| Leasehold Improvements | 129,559 | Net Income | −6,810 |
| Less: Depreciation | −15,449 | Draws | −24,000 |
| *Net Leasehold Improvements* | 114,110 | *YE Michelangelo Equity* | *99,303* |
| *Total Net Tangibles* | 243,201 | **TOTAL MEMBER EQUITY** | **198,606** |
| *Total Fixed Assets* | **254,581** | | |
| *TOTAL ASSETS* | **727,131** | **TOTAL LIABILITIES & EQUITY** | **727,131** |

Part of the reason for this detail is to use some of these statistics for more intense analysis, especially as some of these items relate to the profit and loss statement. Some of that analysis lies in upcoming chapters.

Still, there is information to glean from this revision standing alone. One thing that jumps out immediately is the small cash balance relative to the accounts payable and other current liabilities. This potential cash squeeze represents the most immediate challenge for the owners.

The owners can take some comfort from the large balance of Accounts Receivable, but not too much as those still need to be collected. In fact, their volume suggests that the fact they haven't been collected is the major cause of the looming cash crunch.

Relative to those cash issues, it is interesting that the owners have taken out $48,000 in bonuses on top of salaries and yet Mary is owed $74,000 that she loaned to the Practice while Bob has not loaned any money. Might that prove a source of conflict?

The revised format also indicates that, for the moment, M&B can probably rest easy as far as needing to increase its fixed assets, like equipment, unless it needs to expand capacity.

How do we know? Because the relative portion of each of those fixed asset categories that has been expensed as depreciation is relatively low, suggesting that most of these assets are relatively new and not in need of replacement. If the owners take a closer look at the depreciation schedules then they might see individual assets that are older, but the average age these gross (but no longer raw) figures depict is encouraging on that front.

Hence, if there are to be capital expenditures, perhaps because of new technologies, they can be evaluated on the basis of projected profitability. The other cause could be the need to expand capacity because of greater demand for their services, which would be a positive development (assuming the work is well priced). Those are subjects we'll explore in more detail in Chapters 4 and 5.

## FINANCIAL STATEMENT FORMATTING: THE WHEN

Sloan and Wharton also point out that when additional years and periods of statements are available, it is useful to use a format that compares prior periods with the current period. Those comparisons are best shown on both an absolute basis (i.e. actual dollars) and on a percentage basis. For example, if we take the residential portion of the above statement, we might compare to the prior year (Exhibit 3.5).

What this little matrix shows is cost creep. Other than Employee Benefits with its accelerating health insurance costs, no single figure has climbed outrageously; but the gross margin is being nibbled away by proportionate increases in every direct cost that exceed the increase in revenue. The net result of that is a decline in gross margin; i.e. gross profit as a percentage of revenue.

Sloan jumped on that observation with pointed questions to Bob and Mary: "Did you figure to accept a lower profit rate to attract more revenue? In other words, did you make a calculated decision to reduce your fee to win additional projects, rather than let capacity go idle, so as to increase the overall profit of the Firm? Or is this an unintended outcome? If the latter, there are negative implications to be addressed with managerial action."

Bob responded: "Unfortunately, it never occurred to us. We just proposed and negotiated fees as we always have done."

Sloan and Wharton moved on to another format. Wharton intoned: "That kind of annual comparison is certainly useful at the end of the year, but what about during the year? An additional and valuable interim formatting can also yield information about the future. Let's take a look at the Direct Cost Profit & Loss for the government activity (as it is already refor-matted on the basis of revenue division to examine direct costs and gross profit) as of June 30,[6] halfway through this past year, to see if we can find some more clues to the weakness in the Government line."

---

6   This was included in some of the data that had been provided to Sloan & Wharton, but it is not otherwise reproduced here.

**EXHIBIT 3.5** Profit & Loss Statement: Residential Division

| | Dollar Comparison | | | |
| --- | --- | --- | --- | --- |
| | **Current Year** | **Prior Year** | **Change** | **% Change** |
| Revenue ($) | 638,324 | 603,213 | 35,111 | 5.82 |
| Revenue (%) | 41.28 | 43.58 | −2.30 | |
| | | | | |
| *Variable Costs* | | | | |
| Payroll ($) | 224,591 | 208,814 | 15,777 | 7.56 |
| P/R Taxes ($) | 17,743 | 16,496 | 1,246 | 7.56 |
| Employee Benefits ($) | 27,903 | 21,439 | 6,464 | 30.15 |
| Subcontractors ($) | 108,155 | 96,560 | 11,595 | 12.01 |
| Print & Reproduction ($) | 3,093 | 2,864 | 229 | 8.00 |
| Unreimbursed Travel ($) | 4,045 | 3,230 | 815 | 25.23 |
| Total Variable Costs ($) | 385,530 | 349,403 | 36,127 | 10.34 |
| *Variable Costs (%)* | 60.40 | 57.92 | 2.47 | |
| | | | | |
| Gross Profit ($) | 252,794 | 253,810 | −1,016 | −0.40 |
| *Gross Profit (%)* | 39.60 | 42.08 | −2.47 | |

| | Percentage Comparison | | |
| --- | --- | --- | --- |
| | **Current Year** | **Prior Year** | **% Change** |
| Revenue | 100.00 | 100.00 | 0.00 |
| Revenue | 41.28 | 43.58 | −2.30 |
| | | | |
| *Variable Costs* | | | |
| Payroll | 35.18 | 34.62 | 0.56 |
| P/R Taxes | 2.78 | 2.73 | 0.05 |
| Employee Benefits | 4.37 | 3.55 | 0.82 |
| Subcontractors | 16.94 | 16.01 | 0.93 |
| Print & Reproduction | 0.48 | 0.47 | 0.01 |
| Unreimbursed Travel | 0.63 | 0.54 | 0.09 |
| *Variable Costs* | 60.40 | 57.92 | 2.48 |
| | | | |
| *Gross Profit* | 39.60 | 42.08 | −2.47 |

**EXHIBIT 3.6** Profit & Loss Statement: Government Division

| | 6/30/20XX |
|---|---|
| **Revenue ($)** | **89,860** |
| Revenue (%) | 9.13 |
| | |
| Variable Costs | |
| Payroll ($) | 33,423 |
| Payroll Taxes ($) | 2,640 |
| Employee Benefits ($) | 2,436 |
| Subcontractors ($) | 30,134 |
| Print & Reproduction ($) | 3,668 |
| Unreimbursed Travel ($) | 2,908 |
| Total Variable Costs ($) | **75,209** |
| Variable Costs (%) | 88.81 |
| | |
| **Gross Profit ($)** | **14,651** |
| Gross Profit (%) | 16.30 |

"That's a useful bit of information, showing in particular that the gross profit is pretty ugly," Wharton noted, "but it doesn't tell us very much more. However, if that format had been available to you earlier, it may have alerted you that a problem was brewing." Wharton pulled up another document on his laptop and said, "Imagine if you could have seen this format" (referring to Exhibit 3.7).

The first three columns compare this year's midpoint to the midpoint a year ago and calculate the difference. The fourth column extrapolates the current numbers, so it's simply multiplying the first column's figures by 12 months and dividing by the number of months elapsed; i.e. at the midpoint $12/6 = 2$. (If the calculation was made after, say, 4 months, the multiple would be $12/4 = 3$.) That fourth column is then compared with the year-end numbers for last year.

Extrapolating gives a look into the future. It's not terribly sophisticated but it's a rule of thumb for starters. More sophisticated methods are coming in later chapters.

Wharton's next screen further exploits that format by displaying what Mary and Bob also could have been able to see through the corollary calculation showing line item costs as a percentage of revenue (Exhibit 3.8).

Taking Exhibits 3.7 and 3.8 into account, are there some additional clues here? Yes, indeed! First of all, in the dollar figures of Exhibit 3.7, the dollar revenue is down substantially, calculating to a decline of $24,525/$114,385 or 21.44%. Yet the interesting fact is that if the current level of revenue is maintained (the extrapolation) then M&B would end up ahead of last year's revenues. That's an apparent anomaly to keep in mind.

**EXHIBIT 3.7** Interim Comparison

| Government Division | 6/30/xx | PY 6/30 | Change | Extrapolated | Prior Year | Change |
|---|---|---|---|---|---|---|
| Revenue ($) | **89,860** | **114,385** | **–24,525** | **179,720** | **161,348** | **18,372** |
| *Revenue (%)* | 9.13 | 13.24 | –4.11 | 9.13 | 10.20 | –1.07 |
| | | | | | | |
| *Variable Costs* | | | | | | |
| Payroll ($) | 33,423 | 47,854 | –14,431 | 66,846 | 63,235 | 3,611 |
| Payroll Taxes ($) | 2,640 | 3,780 | –1,140 | 5,281 | 4,996 | 285 |
| Employee Benefits ($) | 2,436 | 3,488 | –1,052 | 4,872 | 4,609 | 263 |
| Subcontractors ($) | 30,134 | 25,764 | 4,370 | 60,268 | 38,250 | 22,018 |
| Print & Reproduction ($) | 3,668 | 4,310 | –642 | 7,336 | 7,112 | 224 |
| Unreimbursed Travel ($) | 2,908 | 3,143 | –235 | 5,816 | 5,230 | 586 |
| *Total Variable Costs ($)* | **75,209** | **88,339** | **–13,130** | **150,419** | **123,431** | **26,987** |
| *Variable Costs (%)* | 83.70 | 77.23 | 6.47 | 83.70 | 76.50 | 7.20 |
| | | | | | | |
| Gross Profit ($) | **14,651** | **26,046** | **–11,395** | **29,301** | **37,917** | **–8,615** |
| *Gross Profit (%)* | 16.30 | 22.77 | –6.47 | 16.30 | 23.50 | –7.20 |

**EXHIBIT 3.8** Costs as a Percentage of Revenue

| | 6/30/xx (%) | PY 6/30 (%) | Change (%) | Extrapolated (%) | Prior Year (%) | Change (%) |
|---|---|---|---|---|---|---|
| Revenue | 100.00 | 100.00 | | 100.00 | 100.00 | |
| | | | | | | |
| *Variable Costs* | | | | | | |
| Payroll | 37.19 | 41.84 | –4.64 | 37.19 | 39.19 | –2.00 |
| Payroll Taxes | 2.94 | 3.31 | –0.37 | 2.94 | 3.10 | –0.16 |
| Employee Benefits | 2.71 | 3.05 | –0.34 | 2.71 | 2.86 | –0.15 |
| Subcontractors | 33.53 | 22.52 | 11.01 | 33.53 | 23.71 | 9.83 |
| Print & Reproduction | 4.08 | 3.77 | 0.31 | 4.08 | 4.41 | –0.33 |
| Unreimbursed Travel | 3.24 | 2.75 | 0.49 | 3.24 | 3.24 | –0.01 |
| *Total Variable Costs* | **83.70** | **77.23** | 6.47 | **83.70** | **76.50** | 7.20 |
| | | | | | | |
| Gross Profit | **16.30** | **22.77** | –6.47 | **16.30** | **23.50** | –7.20 |

Second, per Exhibit 3.7, all of the costs are down except for subcontractors; its figures, apparent in both dollars and percentages, would have been an early warning. That difference really stands out in the extrapolated figures versus last year end.

Third, the gravity of the trouble is accentuated and confirmed by what is happening on the bottom line as profits are dropping off from 22.77% to 16.30%, and if the trend continues, the drop looks to be magnified in the Extrapolation from 23.50% down to 16.30%. That's a proportional decline of

$$(23.50\% - 16.30\%)/23.50\% = 30.64\%!!!$$

And this is a decline in *gross* profit, which is what's left over to help cover all the overhead. Indeed, 16.30% is definitely not much help when the revenue division profit and loss shows Company-wide overhead over the course of the year equaled 46.10% of all revenue!

Sloan now bores in with some conclusions: "What these clues seem to indicate is that as last year wound down, it became apparent that government work was declining since the second half's revenues were down by nearly 60% from last year's first half."

2nd Half Revenue = $161,348 – $114,385 = $47,053

1st Half Revenue % = $114,385/$161,348 = 70.89%

2nd Half Revenue % = $47,053/$161,348 = 20.11%

"In other words, 2nd Half Government Revenue was less than one-third of 1st Half. That's why that anomaly is important—because I bet you saw that decline coming and it led M&B to lower fee standards to secure work. Does that sound right?"

Bob answered: "I kind of quarterbacked the government fee proposals around that time with Richard Watson and Piet Svenson. We were all aware our government backlog was down so we were probably overly optimistic with our numbers."

Wharton took the floor: "Meanwhile, though, it's clear something was seriously amiss in the management of subcontractors for this work. I'm wondering whether that subcontractor problem arose in the fee or the management of subcontractors or in some other way or combination of ways."

Mary's turn: "I ended up being the one to answer the fire alarms and there were way too many. We had to call in subcontractor help because of the time pressures those picky contracting officers put on us. It sure would have been far more beneficial to spot this problem much earlier, which I guess is what this interim formatting would have supported. Lesson learned."

Performing the same analysis on the Practice-wide figures to include the overhead will also offer the same kinds of beneficial insight and is a key point to dealing with Dilemma #4, which will be addressed in detail in the next chapter.

The same kind of comparative analysis, with extrapolative comparisons too, can be performed to compare the current period to the immediately preceding one as well as the same period a year ago. All that's needed is to substitute the prior period for the Year Ago 6/30 figures.

Imagine such comparisons regularly available to managers on a monthly, quarterly and semi-annual basis. In other words, whoever has responsibility for a profit center can benefit from this kind of relatively simple mathematical analysis. Whether it's the Project Manager for a single project (like Zuda or Piet), or Mary taking responsibility for the commercial line of work, or Mary and Bob together looking at the entire Practice. Once the spreadsheet templates are set up, it's easy to plug in the figures and generate the results.

Graphing those results, especially monthly, particularly for the main categories (Revenue, Direct Costs, Gross Profits, Overhead, Net Profits) provides a quick-grasp visual snapshot of how the firm is faring. More will follow in succeeding chapters about analyzing and strategizing over the trends that may be uncovered using that and similar tools.

## WHAT'S NEXT?

We've made a good start on dealing with Dilemma #1, but there's more to consider in the details behind what goes into the financial statements, however they are formatted. As we get a handle on that information, we will see paths to progress and solutions emerging for the other dilemmas that Bob and Mary need to tackle.

**4**

*Data, data, everywhere—
and not a drop to think.*
—with apologies to Samuel
Taylor Coleridge

*Data is not information,
information is not
knowledge, knowledge
is not understanding,
understanding is not
wisdom.*
—Clifford Stoll and
Gary Schubert[1]

# DATA APPLICATION: REFINING ANALYTICS AND CONTROLLING COSTS

## LINE OF ATTACK

After receiving the restated financials along with templates for regular replication, Bob and Mary met a week later with their fearless business consultants Sloan & Wharton, and they began talking again about the state of their business union.

"We need to revisit those Dilemmas," said Bob. "Just

1 www.quotationspage.com/

because we have a clearer picture of where some of the problems lie, doesn't mean the fixes are accomplished or even readily visible. All we've done is pretty much resolve the accounting Dilemma #1 from a macro standpoint, but down deeper we need to figure out how we are going to actually implement changes that will make the Practice more profitable and less stressful—not to mention with more enjoyable and meaningful work."

"Okay," replied Mary, "I say we do this on a triage basis and prioritize to address the most pressing dilemmas. Or on second thought, should we take the one that gives us the biggest benefit? Or on third thought, the one that's easiest to attack so we can get some immediate results?"

Wharton smiled as he said: "Whoa, Mary! I don't think the data has been developed yet to accurately identify how these dilemmas relate to one another or what's easy or most beneficial. That's part of the problem with M&B's data, but that's also what we ought to look at rectifying next. As we do, I think you'll be able to get a feel for those relationships and you two will be able to intuit some of the steps you may want to take. So for now, let's just look at those dilemmas in whatever order your and Bob's instincts seem to suggest."

Mary said: "Well, I keep feeling we could use more revenue, but I know that's going to require spending money, which is tight right now. Maybe we should focus on cost controls?"

"Yes," Bob affirmed, "We've got to conserve cash."

"I think you're on the right track," Wharton said. "But why don't we see first what the cash picture really looks like and then we can examine how we might improve that picture." Bob and Mary both nodded in decisive agreement.

## ROLLING WITH THE CASH FLOW

Wharton continued: "We know your cash balances are low and we know that's our starting point. We have another format that will help: a *rolling cash flow projection*." After asking some questions and reviewing the financial statements, the consultants had a new template completed. Exhibit 4.1 is what Mary and Bob were presented with.

"Oh, Migosh," exclaimed Bob. "We're out of cash within two months! That's even before we make the interim $20,000 payment we need to pay the bank. No more Caribbean retreats! This is disastrous."

Sloan replied: "Well, Bob, this is a first cut; that's why there are those lines at the bottom that provide for financing. Other ways to resolve the problem might include cutting costs or deferring some expenses, which might even include some of your salary payments. It's interesting that it's the second month that's the worst of the three, so if you can get through that then you get some relief from operations in the third month, which would take care of itself. We think, though, there may be an even better solution."

**EXHIBIT 4.1** Rolling Cash Flow Projection

| | Month 1 | Month 2 | Month 3 | Quarter Total |
|---|---|---|---|---|
| OPENING CASH BALANCE | 22,355 | 7,687 | −17,713 | 12,330 |
| *INFLOWS:* | | | | |
| Fee Collections | 114,000 | 106,800 | 136,000 | 356,800 |
| Advance Deposits | 16,200 | 0 | 0 | 16,200 |
| Other | 0 | 1,000 | | 1,000 |
| TOTAL INFLOWS | **130,200** | **107,800** | **136,000** | **374,000** |
| *MANDATORY OUTFLOWS:* | | | | |
| Payroll | 43,916 | 43,916 | 43,916 | 131,748 |
| Subcontractors | 21,350 | 24,880 | 23,000 | 69,230 |
| Rent | 4,240 | 4,360 | 4,360 | 12,960 |
| Tax Deposits | 3,360 | 3,360 | 3,711 | 10,430 |
| Employee Benefits | 0 | 0 | 3,952 | 3,952 |
| Loan Payments | 2,300 | 2,300 | 22,300 | 26,900 |
| Other Job Costs | 11,450 | 10,800 | 10,800 | 33,050 |
| Other Overhead Costs | 35,897 | 35,897 | 35,897 | 107,691 |
| TOTAL MANDATORY OUTFLOWS | **122,513** | **125,513** | **147,936** | **395,961** |
| | | | | |
| NET AVAILABLE CASH | *7,687* | *−17,713* | *−11,936* | *−21,961* |
| | | | | |
| *DISCRETIONARY OUTFLOWS:* | | | | |
| Capital Purchases | 0 | 0 | 0 | 0 |
| Paid to Shareholders | 0 | 0 | 0 | 0 |
| Other Discretionary | 0 | 0 | 0 | 0 |
| TOTAL DISCRETIONARY OUTFLOWS | 0 | 0 | 0 | 0 |
| | | | | |
| PRE-LOAN CASH BALANCE | **7,687** | **−17,713** | **−11,936** | **−21,961** |
| | | | | |
| *LOAN TRANSACTIONS:* | | | | |
| Loans from Banks, etc. | 0 | 0 | 0 | 0 |
| Loans from Shareholders | 0 | 0 | 0 | 0 |
| Less: Loan Prepayments | 0 | 0 | 0 | 0 |
| TOTAL LOAN TRANSACTIONS | 0 | 0 | 0 | 0 |
| | | | | |
| CLOSING LOAN BALANCE | **7,687** | **−17,713** | **−11,936** | **−21,961** |

"Do tell," Mary anxiously pleaded.

Wharton responded to the plea: "We've been looking at your balance sheet and as we indicated in our last meeting, one of the items in which you have a lot of money tied up is receivables. If we can help you accelerate some of those into collections, that could solve this problem. If we can help you systematize that, and we think we can, it may well clear one of your dilemmas—Collections, #13—and maybe help with two others—your Personal Incomes, #9 and Financing, #2."

Back to Alfred: "Before we do that, though, we want to stress that this kind of rolling cash flow projection is another template you should be using regularly. It ought to be refined down to a week-by-week or even daily projection, and before we're through here today, we're going to give you some tips on how it is easily monitored. On top of that, it should be used to look further out. Here's what I tentatively think would be ideal, given our familiarity with the construction industry."

**EXHIBIT 4.2** Rolling Cash Budget Time Lines

| Periodicity | Length | Comments |
| --- | --- | --- |
| Daily | 7 Days | To cover the coming week |
| Weekly | 5 Weeks | Five weeks in order to cover a full month ahead |
| Monthly | 6 Months | Monthly tends to be the key strategic tool |
| Quarterly | 4 Quarters | Projecting one year is logical, especially for financing |
| Yearly | 5 Years | Optional, as may be too speculative |

Sloan continued: "Each of these would get updated after each period expires. So the daily one gets updated after each day, the weekly one after each week, etc. The computer should make it pretty easy to do that functionally, *but* it means someone has to know what's going on with the Firm so that the input is accurate; otherwise it's misleading. And someone with decisional authority, probably one of you two, has to look at this periodically, and whoever is prepping these templates should understand you need to be alerted if the numbers are signaling trouble, as they are in this run. If nobody pays timely attention to what it says, it's just a waste of time."

Bob swallowed hard. "Since I've kind of become Chief Administrator, that's probably more demands on my time. Pretty scary."

"Maybe, but if you can get this right, I bet it will save you a lot of time in the future," Sloan retorted. "And, I'd add that we think most of the preparation effort should be a subordinate's job. For now, though, let's divert to our analysis of the Accounts Receivable."

# RECEIVABLES ANALYSIS

Sloan and Wharton then presented an interesting statistic about the Accounts Receivable (AcctsR). The Average Age of Receivables evidences the length of time it takes to collect the average dollar of fees:

(AcctsR/Revenues) $\times$ 365 days

($388,955/$1,546,141) $\times$ 365 = 91.82 days

M&B's contracts and invoices stated payment was due in 30 days for residential clients and 45 days for commercial and governmental clients. Given the blend of revenues, the average time should have equaled about 39 days [((41.28% $\times$ 30) + (58.82% $\times$ 45))/100 = 38.85 days].

Hence, it's taking (91.82/38.85) = 2.36 times as long to get paid as it should, according to M&B's policies.

Sloan and Wharton's next step was to break down the receivables into five categories based on arrearage (Exhibit 4.3).

The two oldest columns showed the problem isn't due to some single account outlier skewing the average but, rather, that collections were abysmal with well over half of the accounts being more than 15 days late. That opened another avenue of inquiry, leading to an expansion of this table (Exhibit 4.4).

**EXHIBIT 4.3** Receivables Based on Arrearage

| <30 Days | 30–44 Days | 45–59 Days | 60–89 Days | >90 Days | Total |
|---|---|---|---|---|---|
| $77,345 | $38,354 | $59,621 | $134,811 | $78,824 | $388,955 |
| 19.89% | 9.86% | 15.33% | 34.66% | 20.27% | 100.00% |

**EXHIBIT 4.4** Receivables Based on Arrearage and Project Categories

| Days | Residential ($) | (%) | Commercial ($) | (%) | Government ($) | (%) | Total ($) |
|---|---|---|---|---|---|---|---|
| <30 | 18,544 | 4.77 | 44,154 | 11.35 | 14,647 | 3.77 | 77,345 |
| 30–44 | 4,018 | 1.03 | 27,100 | 6.97 | 7,236 | 1.86 | 38,354 |
| 45–59 | 6,013 | 1.55 | 43,988 | 11.31 | 9,620 | 2.47 | 59,621 |
| 60–89 | 41,784 | 10.74 | 31,682 | 8.15 | 61,345 | 15.77 | 134,811 |
| >90 | 44,890 | 11.54 | 31,314 | 8.05 | 2,620 | 0.67 | 78,824 |
| Total | 115,249 | 29.63 | 178,238 | 45.82 | 95,468 | 24.54 | 388,955 |
| Revenue | 638,324 | | 719,381 | | 188,436 | | 1,546,141 |
| Mid Avg | 92.00 | | 61.93 | | 62.67 | | 71.02 |

Note: Sum Percent Totals may not sum exactly due to rounding.

**EXHIBIT 4.5** Receivables Based on Arrearage and Project Categories, Weighted Average

| Days | Midpt Day | Wtd Avg Residential | Wtd Avg Commercial | Wtd Avg Government | All Wtd Avg |
|---|---|---|---|---|---|
| <30 | 14.5 | 2.33 | 3.59 | 2.22 | 2.88 |
| 30–44 | 37.5 | 1.31 | 5.70 | 2.84 | 3.70 |
| 45–59 | 52.5 | 2.74 | 12.96 | 5.29 | 8.05 |
| 60–89 | 75.0 | 27.19 | 13.33 | 48.19 | 25.99 |
| >90 | 150.0 | 58.43 | 26.35 | 4.12 | 30.40 |
| Total | 329.5 | 92.00 | 61.93 | 62.67 | 71.02 |

All of the invoice ages have been categorized and summed, and the percentage of the grand total of receivables has been calculated. Additionally, the revenue has been included for comparison's sake. Exhibit 4.4 has also permitted a more detailed calculation of average age for each of the three business lines, so Exhibit 4.5 has been calculated by a weighted average method, explained in detail below.

The methodology used was to first determine the midpoint in each age group. For >90, a figure of 150 days was chosen. Then that midpoint was multiplied by the fraction each category represented of all the receivables for that line item in the preceding Exhibit 4.4. (Example: *Wtd. Avg. Residential* in the row <30 days: 14.5 × (18,544/115,249) = 2.33)

The numbers in each column above were then summed and that sum was then divided by the total number of midpoint days; i.e. by 329.5. Other than for purposes of making the calculation, only the bottom figure matters in each column and those figures have been inserted as the bottom row in the preceding Exhibit 4.4.

Lastly, a percentages table for each of those categories was also computed (Exhibit 4.6).

As an example to be sure the meaning of Exhibit 4.6 is clear, residential receivables less than 30 days old equal 23.98% of all receivables less than 30 days old.

**EXHIBIT 4.6** Receivables Based on Arrearage and Project Categories, by Percentages

| Days | Residential ($) | Residential (%) | Commercial ($) | Commercial (%) | Government ($) | Government (%) | Total ($) |
|---|---|---|---|---|---|---|---|
| <30 | 18,544 | 23.98 | 44,154 | 57.09 | 14,647 | 18.94 | 77,345 |
| 30–44 | 4,018 | 10.48 | 27,100 | 70.66 | 7,236 | 18.87 | 38,354 |
| 45–59 | 6,013 | 10.09 | 43,988 | 73.78 | 9,620 | 16.14 | 59,621 |
| 60–89 | 41,784 | 30.99 | 31,682 | 23.50 | 61,345 | 45.50 | 134,811 |
| >90 | 44,890 | 56.95 | 31,314 | 39.73 | 2,620 | 3.32 | 78,824 |
| Total | 115,249 | 29.63 | 178,238 | 45.82 | 95,468 | 24.54 | 388,955 |
| Revenue | 638,324 | 41.28 | 719,381 | 46.53 | 188,436 | 12.19 | 1,546,142 |

"Great," said Bob. "What is this telling us?"

Sloan responded: "Several points. Let's start with Exhibit 4.6 and work backwards. First, note where the big numbers are. The really reprehensible numbers are the ones over 90 days and more than half of those are with your residential clients, with some commercial clients not far behind. That small $2,620 of government money is probably hung up over some dispute or invoicing flaw. If you just collected half of that $78,824, the crisis is averted.

"Second, that next batch, the 60–89 day group, is the largest and also all overdue. Of that, my bet is you'll soon see most if not all of that government money; as we know governments tend to pay within 90 days regardless of the contract terms. So that $61,345 is going to likely give you some relief, but without this analysis, it might well just mask the problem.

"Third, if we look at those preceding two Exhibits (4.4 and 4.5) together, that mid-point average accentuates how the residential clients are really causing you trouble with your cash flow."

"You know," Mary thoughtfully interjected, "So many of those residential jobs are relatively small and so it would be labor-intensive to chase those. Jan just doesn't have the time, especially if she's going to be even busier doing all those additional reports . . ."

Bob nodded in obvious agreement and then, with a look of puzzled concern, stammered: "But, but . . . we need the money. Badly. Do you guys have a solution?"

"We've got no magic wands, but we're not destitute of ideas," Wharton said reassuringly. "This issue is one point to consider in whether you add an administrator. We'll come back to that.

"If these are all solid clients, some notes, calls, emails, and social media chatter with them may be all you need to get paid. It's generally true that 'the squeaky wheel gets the grease' when it comes to collecting receivables."

Sloan and Wharton then offered a menu of ideas to prompt payment for new projects:

- **Pre-bill.** Send invoices before the work is done and be sure your contract permits that, particularly for fixed fee jobs. The longer a bill hangs around, the more likely it is to get paid.

- **Frequent billing.** Make sure your contract allows you to bill more frequently, perhaps twice a month. Don't let big numbers build up; after all, you are paying out payroll twice a month.

- **Charge for late payments.** Include a late fee and start charging interest. Be sure to check with your lawyer on what you have to disclose and how much interest you can charge. Federal and state laws create a patchwork of limitations, especially when dealing with consumers such as your residential clients. But being able to charge interest and late fees—and actually doing it—will hasten payment and compensate you for delay. Plus, that's a bargaining chip you can negotiate away if you need to actively collect.

- **Attorney fees.** Be sure your contract lets you collect attorney fees if you have to sue to collect. That's another cudgel to wave if clients are slow payers.

- **Quick-pay discounts.** For really fast payment (e.g. 7 or 10 days), offer a discount. A standard quick-pay discount is 1% or 2% but you may want to go somewhat higher, keeping in mind that discounts theoretically equate to an interest rate on your money. For example, if you give a 1% discount for payment within 10 days when the bill is due in 30 days, that's 20 days for 1%, which works out to $(365/20) \times 1\% = 18.25\%$. It's theoretical because the real cost is the blended rate of those that take the discount but would pay when due averaged with those it incentivizes to pay earlier rather than late. Anyway, a payment discount can also be used as a selling point when you're making proposals. If it brings in your money faster, it may well be worth it in stress reduction and time savings, as long as your jobs are priced right from inception—pricing is the key. If you adopt this strategy, just be sure to police it so clients don't knock off the discount and still pay late. That's where the late charge and interest can be an added plus.

- **Work suspension.** Also make sure you can stop work, with short notice too, if your client falls behind in payments. That usually proves a very powerful right in commercial deals.

- **Work product ownership.** Another legal point to include in your standard contract is a provision that the client does not receive ownership of, or license to use, any of the work product until and unless all fees are fully paid. Again, for the commercial clients, that's a powerful point as a reminder for any recalcitrant payer.

Sloan and Wharton acknowledged that it was unlikely that most of these terms could be used for government contracts with their regulatory overlay, but that would not mean that any governmental slow-pay should be immune from hortatory communications.

Bob stroked his chin as he contemplated the menu. "Well, that is interesting," he said. "But you know we're in a very competitive location and not in the best economy. We really have to make strenuous efforts to attract business. I'm not at all sure all of that legal stuff is going to fly. It may well scare some people away."

Wharton looked straight into Bob's eyes and said: "There are twin responses, Bob. First, what good is getting work if you are not going to be paid for it, or not fairly paid? Second, and I'm not being flippant when I say this, salesmanship is making the client intent on hiring you. None—and I stress that word, *none*—of these terms should be a problem *if* the client is paying on time. That's your pitch. If the client can't accept that, then why strain your capacity, your staff, and yourself working to satisfy someone who is not going to fairly compensate you? Payment when due is half of fair compensation."

Bob and Mary exchanged glances. Some doubt was still evident, but the logic was awfully hard to ignore. "Let's assume that's right," said Mary. "We can always back off if we think that's the right thing to do." Bob smiled. "The truth hurts only when it should."

# IMPACT OF COLLECTIONS

Sloan wanted to steer the conversation back on point: "We were looking at that rolling cash flow projection before we detoured for the important receivables issue. Taking that all into account, if you concentrate on going after the residential and commercial receivables over the next several weeks, what's your conservative estimate of the portion of these older receivables you can collect?"

Bob looked at Mary and replied: "If we do it with the right touch, so as to not alienate our clients, I honestly think we can pull in 60%—yes, I said *60%*—of the amounts due that are at least 60 days old. Do you agree, Mary?"

Mary said: "Well, that's going to steal some time from marketing and networking, but we must get paid for the work we do. I think that is a conservative number."

"Okay then," said Wharton. "Give me a moment and I can integrate those numbers into the template. An extra line (Fee Collections—Arrearages) is added in Exhibit 4.7 for those collection efforts and I highlighted that line in gray." Exhibit 4.7 shows the spreadsheet he produced.

**EXHIBIT 4.7** Rolling Cash Flow Budget with Fee Collections—Arrearages

|  | Month 1 | Month 2 | Month 3 | Quarter Total |
|---|---|---|---|---|
| OPENING CASH BALANCE | 22,355 | 97,489 | 57,278 | 177,122 |
| *INFLOWS:* | | | | |
| Fee Collections—Current | 114,000 | 106,800 | 136,000 | 356,800 |
| Fee Collections—Arrearages | 89,802 | 91,346 | 58,291 | 239,439 |
| Advance Deposits | 16,200 | 61,345 | 0 | 77,545 |
| Other | 0 | 1,000 | 0 | 1,000 |
| TOTAL INFLOWS | **220,002** | **260,491** | **194,291** | **674,784** |
| *MANDATORY OUTFLOWS:* | | | | |
| Payroll | 43,916 | 43,916 | 43,916 | 131,748 |
| Subcontractors | 21,350 | 24,880 | 23,000 | 69,230 |
| Rent | 4,240 | 4,360 | 4,360 | 12,960 |
| Tax Deposits * | 3,360 | 3,360 | 3,711 | 10,430 |
| Employee Benefits | 0 | 0 | 3,952 | 3,952 |
| Loan Payments | 2,300 | 2,300 | 22,300 | 26,900 |
| Other Job Costs | 11,450 | 10,800 | 10,800 | 33,050 |
| Other Overhead Costs | 35,897 | 35,897 | 35,897 | 107,691 |
| TOTAL MANDATORY OUTFLOWS | 122,513 | 125,513 | 147,936 | 395,961 |
| NET AVAILABLE CASH | **97,489** | **134,978** | **46,355** | **278,823** |

**EXHIBIT 4.7** *continued*

|  | Month 1 | Month 2 | Month 3 | Quarter Total |
|---|---|---|---|---|
| *DISCRETIONARY OUTFLOWS:* | | | | |
| Capital Purchases | 0 | 0 | 0 | 0 |
| Paid to Shareholders | 0 | 0 | 0 | 0 |
| Other Discretionary | 0 | 0 | 0 | 0 |
| TOTAL DISCRETIONARY OUTFLOWS | 0 | 0 | 0 | 0 |
| | | | | |
| PRE-LOAN CASH BALANCE | **97,489** | **134,978** | **46,355** | **278,823** |
| | | | | |
| *LOAN TRANSACTIONS:* | | | | |
| Loans from Banks, etc. | 0 | 0 | 0 | 0 |
| Loans from Shareholders | 0 | −77,700 | 0 | −77,700 |
| Less: Loan Prepayments | 0 | 0 | 0 | 0 |
| TOTAL LOAN TRANSACTIONS | 0 | −77,700 | 0 | −77,700 |
| | | | | |
| CLOSING LOAN BALANCE | **97,489** | **57,278** | **46,355** | **201,123** |

Note: * Tax Deposits do not include federal, state or local income taxes. See Chapter 6 "Other Constraints."

Bob and Mary both seemed to exhale simultaneously. "Wow," said Bob. "Fantastic," said Mary. "What an incredible difference. Is this really possible? Could my loan even be paid off?"

Wharton replied: "*If* M&B can really make that kind of progress on working down receivables, it can be done. Of course, you've got to accomplish that while you're still priming the pump with new work. It's analogous to the cliché that you must do the most effective marketing when you are busiest."

Bob seemed determined when he said: "Mary, I'm fairly certain I can handle the collections. When I do, I'd really appreciate it if you'd acknowledge that my administrative oversight has a value too. I'm so glad this offers a way to pay back your loan. I still feel badly that Sally and I have been so strapped paying for college for two kids at the same time. The way you stepped up by loaning that money when we really needed it literally saved the Firm. I am very lucky to have you as my business partner. I know it's been tense sometimes, but this could be a breakthrough moment for us. And Alfred and Joseph, if we can make this work, I can't wait to see what else you've got in your bag of tricks."

# DIRECT COST CONTROLS

"I'm beginning to wonder, Bob," said Sloan, "if you are psychic because I've got another set of tricks that I think may just knock your socks off."

"Psychic or psychotic?" Mary added with a hint of sarcasm.

"No comment," Sloan smiled in reply. "And, to quote the late Senator Leverett Saltonstall, 'That's off the record.'" He paused, then said: "Seriously though, let's address those direct costs. Do you realize that if you can lower those, which raises your gross margin, it has kind of a multiplier effect. 'How so?' you might ask. It's because you need correspondingly less revenue to cover expenditures.

"If you can increase M&B's gross margin by a material percentage, it can be very beneficial. Let's pretend you could cut your direct costs by 10%, or you could cut overhead by the same number of dollars. The top half of Exhibit 4.8 shows a base case and the effect of those two alternatives.

"Now, assume you can hold those relationships while revenues increase 10%. The bottom half of Exhibit 4.8 shows the effect of the two alternatives in the next period with higher revenues. The middle column shows the new direct cost *percentage* applying to those rev-

**EXHIBIT 4.8** Direct Cost Reduction v. Overhead Reduction

|              | Base Case | | Lower Direct Costs | | Lower Overhead | |
|--------------|---------|---------|---------|---------|---------|---------|
|              | ($) | (%) | ($) | (%) | ($) | (%) |
| Revenue      | 1,000 | 100.0 | 1,000 | 100.0 | 1,000 | 100.0 |
| Direct Costs | 600 | 60.0 | 540 | 54.0 | 600 | 60.0 |
| Gross Profit | 400 | 40.0 | 460 | 46.0 | 400 | 40.0 |
| Overhead     | 350 | 35.0 | 350 | 35.0 | 290 | 29.0 |
| Net Profit   | 50 | 5.0 | 110 | 11.0 | 110 | 11.0 |
| *+10% Rev.*  | | | | | | |
| Revenue      | 1,100 | 110.0 | 1,100 | 110.0 | 1,100 | 110.0 |
| Direct Costs | 660 | 66.0 | 594 | 59.4 | 660 | 66.0 |
| Gross Profit | 440 | 44.0 | 506 | 50.6 | 440 | 44.0 |
| Overhead     | 350 | 35.0 | 350 | 35.0 | 290 | 29.0 |
| Net Profit   | 90 | 9.0 | 156 | 15.6 | 150 | 15.0 |

enues, but with the unreduced overhead from the base case. The third column shows the reduced level of overhead with the new commissions, but with the unchanged direct cost *percentage*. The profit is higher as a result of establishing a lower direct cost regime rather than setting a lower overhead level."

Wharton chimed in: "If revenue was dropping, the overhead savings would matter more. This example demonstrates the effect when revenue is rising, which is what you are expecting. Maybe we can help you achieve the ideal situation of reductions in both without compromising revenue. So let's look at those direct costs. As we saw in our last meeting, there are two problems: subcontractor expenses out of control and cost creep across the board."

## COMPARING PROPOSAL TO BUDGET

Wharton kept talking and pointed out that fundamental to crafting any work proposal to a client is an estimate of the cost to complete the work. That estimate should also constitute a budget for the project once the work is awarded. If the proposal gets tweaked, the budget needs to be tweaked as well.

Someone must be assigned as project manager. Just as important as the goal of completing the work is the goal of completing it within budgeted fee. The project manager has to understand this concept. In fact, this concept must be inculcated as a fundamental element of the Practice's philosophy. The skillful manager is the one who can deliver top quality within the constraints of the fee-driven budget.

Obviously, that includes controlling the costs for subcontractors, and one of the questions about those costs is, "What's the source of the cost overruns?" To answer that question, there seem to be three possible differentiators that can be examined to isolate the source (or maybe sources):

1. subcontractor specialty (i.e. engineer, landscape architect, interior designer, etc.);

2. Project Manager;

3. project type (i.e. residential, commercial, or governmental).

One good analytical method looks at all your projects within discrete periods—month, quarter, year—with all three of those attributes duly organized. The place to start is to guess which of those three differentiators is the most likely culprit. Let's assume it's the project manager and set up a series of matrices, one for each of the project managers (Exhibit 4.9).

Once that analysis is run, it may indicate the project manager is not the critical differentiator, and you may still be able to see that one of the other differentiators is the primary source of the cost overrun; but if it's still murky, you can reconfigure the analysis to look like Exhibit 4.10 or Exhibit 4.11.

**EXHIBIT 4.9** Fee Analysis as a Function of Project Manager (PM)

| PM:_____ | | Engineer | | Landscape Architect | | Interior Designer | | All Subcontractors | |
|---|---|---|---|---|---|---|---|---|---|
| | | ($) | (%) | ($) | (%) | ($) | (%) | ($) | (%) |
| Residential | Budget | | | | | | | | |
| | Actual | | | | | | | | |
| | Variance | | | | | | | | |
| Commercial | Budget | | | | | | | | |
| | Actual | | | | | | | | |
| | Variance | | | | | | | | |
| Government | Budget | | | | | | | | |
| | Actual | | | | | | | | |
| | Variance | | | | | | | | |
| TOTAL | Budget | | | | | | | | |
| | Actual | | | | | | | | |
| | Variance | | | | | | | | |

**EXHIBIT 4.10** Fee Analysis as a Function of Project Type

| Residential | | Engineer | | Landscape Architect | | Interior Designer | | All Subcontractors | |
|---|---|---|---|---|---|---|---|---|---|
| | | ($) | (%) | ($) | (%) | ($) | (%) | ($) | (%) |
| Zuda | Budget | | | | | | | | |
| | Actual | | | | | | | | |
| | Variance | | | | | | | | |
| Richard | Budget | | | | | | | | |
| | Actual | | | | | | | | |
| | Variance | | | | | | | | |
| Mary | Budget | | | | | | | | |
| | Actual | | | | | | | | |
| | Variance | | | | | | | | |
| Bob | Budget | | | | | | | | |
| | Actual | | | | | | | | |
| | Variance | | | | | | | | |
| TOTAL | Budget | | | | | | | | |
| | Actual | | | | | | | | |
| | Variance | | | | | | | | |

**EXHIBIT 4.11** Fee Analysis as a Function of Subcontractor Specialty

| Structural Engineer | | Residential | | Commercial | | Government | | All Subcontractors | |
|---|---|---|---|---|---|---|---|---|---|
| | | ($) | (%) | ($) | (%) | ($) | (%) | ($) | (%) |
| Zuda | Budget | | | | | | | | |
| | Actual | | | | | | | | |
| | Variance | | | | | | | | |
| Richard | Budget | | | | | | | | |
| | Actual | | | | | | | | |
| | Variance | | | | | | | | |
| Mary | Budget | | | | | | | | |
| | Actual | | | | | | | | |
| | Variance | | | | | | | | |
| Bob | Budget | | | | | | | | |
| | Actual | | | | | | | | |
| | Variance | | | | | | | | |
| TOTAL | Budget | | | | | | | | |
| | Actual | | | | | | | | |
| | Variance | | | | | | | | |

Sloan added that there may not be any consistency in causation. If that's the case then at least Mary and Bob know the focus has to be job by job. If there is consistency, there may be some broader cure that can be put in place. For example, if the cause is one project manager then some additional training and oversight for both the proposal and the performance duties are in order.

However, this initial analysis may require drilling deeper into the cause. For example, if it's one subcontractor specialty, is that specialty dominated by one consultant, and if so, should the Practice be searching for some competitors? Or if it's one project type, is there some aspect of that work that seems to be primarily generating these extra costs?

There could be other factors that deserve consideration—project distance from M&B's office comes to mind as an example—so there may be other differentiators to substitute in the matrix.

"Now that's the strategic overview," Wharton summarized, "telling you *where* to look and *what* to look out for; but it doesn't automatically control those direct costs. Controlling costs is easy to state but not so easy in practice. In fact, it's really hard if your project managers are not supplied with the critical tools to exercise that control."

Having the fee proposal become a budget is one leg of the tripod on which cost control stands; the other two legs are monitoring and enforcing that budget. There is one key tool for each of those other two legs, respectively, *Timely Organized Data* and *Flexible Contracts*. The consultants describe those in the next two sections.

## TIMELY ORGANIZED DATA

The budget for the total fee has to be monitored. If there are change orders, the budget should be updated. The cost creep issue and the subcontractor overruns can be controlled only when action is taken by a project manager or a principal to hold costs in check.

Clearly, like dealing with cancer, early detection is the watchword. Early detection requires rapid capture and frequent reporting of actual results. That effort requires the right technology and adequate manpower. We'll look at those constraints in a later chapter, but there are some other considerations to the budget question to make it work as an early warning system so threats to profitability can be addressed sooner rather than later.

The typical proposal is calculated using the inputs and their concomitant dollar costs over the course of the entire project. Such costs rarely, if ever, are incurred ratably. Rather, the inputs are naturally sporadic, and to complicate the matter, some activities are dependent on others and some are interdependent.

As referenced in our subcontractor analysis matrix (Exhibit 4.10), the baseline calculation is

Budget – Actual = Variance

That may be fine at the end of a project, but while the project is moving forward, those numbers are not likely to be accurately revealing if the timing for expenses is not accounted for. Hence, every project's proposal development should include a forecast of the timing for when the inputs will be utilized and when the costs will be recognized and when they will be paid, that last point being a key consideration for cash flow. All of those points should be coordinated with the client payments so as to yield a cushion on cash flow.

Using a Critical Path Method (CPM) Program in developing and tracking each proposal is perhaps the easiest way to get such a budget put together and monitored.

## FLEXIBLE CONTRACTS

If monitoring signals that there is a problem, what's to be done to get a project and its costs back on course? Most of those costs are going to be laborcentric: either staff time or subcontractor time. Let's deal with the latter first.

A crucial determinant for controlling subcontractor costs is the contract itself between the Practice and the subcontractor. The right terms can provide the Practice with the flexibility it may need to make changes as a project's peculiarities unfold. Mary and Bob should be pushing each subcontractor to accept a standard AIA contract that contains the following terms:

- **Fixed Price.** Ordinarily, a fixed price contract is preferable because of the certainty it provides, putting the risk of overages on the subcontractor; although without the next six provisions, it can turn out to be disadvantageous.

- **Work Adjustment.** The Practice needs the right to change the work if circumstances change—of course, with a reasonable negotiated adjustment to price, up or down.

- **Suspension Right.** If a client is not making payments when due or other circumstances intervene (e.g. acts of God) that might make it desirable or necessary to suspend work then it's critical that, at your direction, the subcontractor will also suspend work and charges without penalty.

- **Cancellation Right.** Similarly, if a project is terminated by the client (presumably in accord with contract) or by the Practice (e.g. on account of client failure to pay) then the contract with the subcontractor has to be automatically terminated without penalty.

- **Termination Right.** Separately, the Practice ought to have a right to terminate the contract without penalty for cause, meaning if the subcontractor breaches the contract. A clear definition of subcontractor duties and of breaches is critical. In an ideal world, the Practice would be able to terminate for convenience (i.e. not for cause) at any time without penalty; but such an arrangement is, indeed, idealistic, except perhaps when dealing with freelancers. Turnover to you of data, work in progress, ownership rights, etc. should be a part of any such termination.

- **Substitution Right.** If the contract is terminated because of a failure of the subcontractor, the Practice should be able not only to substitute another subcontractor but also to charge back the dismissed subcontractor for all extra costs resulting from the need to substitute.

- **Withholding Right.** Additionally, if there is a termination, the Practice should be able to offset money owed for a breach and costs incurred in substitution from the terminated subcontractor.

- **Expense Approval.** The subcontractor should not be able to incur any other expenses that would be charged to the Practice without prior approval. However, there may be circumstances in which delay caused by approval could be troublesome, so an alternative is to set one or more limits and require approval for exceeding those limits.

- **Waiver of Lien Rights.** Apart from the project in which the client's bargaining power has forced the Practice to waive, the reason a waiver of lien rights from a subcontractor is desirable is to avoid problems and embarrassment with the client if a dispute with the subcontractor leads the Practice to withhold payment.

- **Periodic Reporting.** To make monitoring efficient, the subcontractor has to be required to submit frequent, periodic, and accurate reports on work performed as a condition of getting paid. While meetings might be expected to produce similar information, the advantage is in transferring information directly to those analyzing.

- **Data Match.** Further to that point, setting forth in the contract *how* information is transmitted, both in form and medium (i.e. electronic), to facilitate the Practice's own record-keeping and analysis can save time and increase efficiency and transparency. As more and more clients demand exactly that cooperation, it becomes inevitable that the Practice must do likewise by those serving it.

- **Correction Duty.** Where errors are due to the subcontractor, a standard should be imposed for correction within a specific (or Practice-definable) time and without cost to the Practice. Tying in the above Withholding Right and Termination Right will give more teeth to this provision.

- **Pay When Paid.** A terrific term to obtain is one in which payment is not due to the sub-contractor until the Practice has collected the corresponding payment from the client. Obviously, that can be a huge palliative for cash flow. Admittedly, this is often not easy to get.

Of course, these terms are largely emblematic of a zero-sum relationship in which the sub-contractor is going to be looking for the opposite stance, so that the negotiations over the contract determine what the final deal looks like. Bargaining power is critical.

But more critical is the underlying relationship of the parties. There is no substitute for a relationship of reciprocal trust and mutual goodwill in which the parties are working toward the common goal of an on-time—and of course, high-quality—delivery. Contracts that effectively incentivize all parties to strive together and cooperate with one another are the most desirable.

## THE COMPENSATION PUZZLE

Walking briskly back to the office after a healthy lunch of salads and S. Pellegrino, the two partners and their business consultants broached the pivotal topic of compensation. What follows is the executive summary of what the Practice is doing now (including many typical mistakes) and Sloan and Wharton's insights into creating an innovative new compensation program that has potential to greatly benefit both the Practice and its staff.

The single biggest cost remains compensation of its staff. The cost of that compensation also includes not only the base pay itself plus any bonuses but all the add-ons of payroll overhead. The list of those add-ons, a growing number of which have become mandatory for employers, may well include:

- Employer's Share of FICA (Social Security) Tax*^

- Employer's Share of Medicare Tax*

- Federal Unemployment Tax\*^

- State Unemployment Tax\*^

- Worker Compensation Insurance\*

- Comprehensive Liability Insurance

- Professional's Malpractice Insurance>

- Health Insurance><

- Disability Insurance<

- Life Insurance<

- Leave Pay (Sick, Vacation, Family Medical, etc.)><

- Retirement Plan Contributions<

---

**Key:**

\* Mandatory

> Mandatory in some jurisdictions or for certain employer characteristics (e.g. number of employees)

^ Percentage of payroll up to certain levels of payroll

< Not applicable to part-time and casual employees; and may be subject to waiting period

---

Other benefits (e.g. tuition assistance, continuing education costs, license and/or exam fee reimbursement, professional association membership, etc.) might further add to the costs of maintaining statutory employees. That list also does not include the human resource management costs implicit in such maintenance, from payroll processing to insurance management. Such costs typically are subsumed—often imperceptibly—in one or more overhead accounts.

No doubt, the recitation of all those costs gives most employers pause when the subject of adding staff arises. They also increase the temptation to use contractor individuals and part-timers instead, despite the lesser degree of control and the implicit risks of divided loyalty and disloyalty. (See discussion of the virtual office in Chapter 7.)

Of all the dilemmas that Bob and Mary are facing, none seems more of a conundrum than that of staff retention. Why? Because none of the others seem to harbor the following inherent contradicting tensions:

- If people aren't paid enough, they will leave; but if people are paid too much, the Practice loses clients or money, or both.

- Even when people are well paid, or even overpaid, they may still leave.

- Retaining a hierarchy of pay grades is expected; but that rewards position, not performance.

- The nature of the profession is such that people are typically paid before (often long before) the client pays for their services.

- It's much easier to hire in the face of increasing demand than to terminate employees in the face of declining demand.

- It's natural to expect that longevity and seniority will mean more pay, but that does not necessarily translate into more profitable performance.

Right now, M&B utilizes a standard compensation model. Professionals and upper-level employees receive a standard salary paid every two weeks. Lower-level employees are paid based on hours worked at a set hourly rate and are also paid every two weeks. Once a year toward year end, Mary and Bob get together to award Holiday bonuses based on what the Practice has earned for the year, how much cash they have on hand, and the subjective feelings of Mary and Bob about what is "fair" for each employee given the employee's position in the Practice hierarchy, seniority, and perceived performance. In the same vein, once a year for each employee, around the time of the employment anniversary, Bob and Mary get together and decide how much of an increase in pay is "fair" for the employee, considering most of the same factors as well as how the near-term picture looks for the Practice.

This model is fraught with a number of shortcomings because of its subjectivity. Employees may not really be treated fairly because the perceptions may be skewed at any one time by any of those factors—even including whether Bob or Mary are feeling happy or unhappy at the moment they are to make a decision. Worse, in today's world, the perception that some kind of discrimination is being practiced creates a danger both for morale and for the pocketbook. Employees may well not share the same subjective view of their own performance so that retention of good employees may be harder to achieve—and morale may suffer. On top of all that, Bob and Mary are fundamentally *guessing* how much they should deprive the Practice and themselves in order to try to satisfy employee demand for ever higher pay.

Is there a better way?

Imagine a compensation program that is performance based, not merely time based. Such a program would be transparent to the employee so that the employee could understand how performance translates to the employee's own paychecks. It would also be transparent to Bob and Mary so they can evaluate whether the replacement of an employee is preferable to retention. It would be so designed to provide the Practice with the internally generated capital it needs to grow and would conserve capital during tougher times. It would automatically incentivize good performance and penalize poor performance. It would not be complicated to implement, manage, or explain. It would not be so radical as to scare away any employee or recruit. It would be objectively fair.

Here is just such a design. There is a base salary (or hourly wage). There are *quarterly* bonuses available to employees, calculated as follows:

- A minimum cash profit must be earned by the Practice for the quarter.

- A minimum cash balance must be on hand when bonuses are due to be paid.

- A portion of the cash profit above the minimum goes into a pool, which is shared using a point system for employees.

- The point system is a function of a few objective metrics for each position.

- The points are further adjusted by a "position constant" to recognize the hierarchical importance of different positions and to incentivize advancement.

- Bonuses are then awarded based on each employee's adjusted points as a percentage of the total number of points.

- Bonuses are paid 45 days after the close of the quarter (to give enough time to confirm calculation) *and* the employee must be employed on that date to receive the bonus.

Why a *quarterly* bonus? An annual or semiannual bonus is unlikely to offer enough incentive throughout the year and potentially encourages employees to "hang around" to get last year's bonus and then quit. On the other hand, a monthly bonus is likely to be too small to encourage an employee to stay on. Further, a month is too short a time period to incentivize sustained positive performance.

Here's an example using Richard Watson, one of the Project Managers. He has been the highest paid employee (apart from the owners) with a current salary of $72,000. From Chapter 2, it may be recalled that he has a history of alienating employees and clients, a trait that Mary and Bob would like to try to moderate while not losing the valuable experience that Richard contributes. Similarly, Zuda, the other Project Manager, has also had problems with clients because of her inexperience. That will play into the metrics that we are designing *by position*.

In order to make this program work, let's assume that we want to send a message to all employees that this is not just a new benefit piled on the others but, rather, it's a major shift in philosophy and intended to be an integral part of everyone's compensation. Accordingly, we want to *reduce base salaries* for everyone by 10%. For Richard, this means a reduction in his *base salary* to $64,800 per year or $16,200 per quarter, a reduction of $1,800 for the quarter. This step is going to take some diplomatic effort as it must be true for Richard and everyone else that every employee is well positioned to earn more, and each must be convinced of that.

So here's the calculation of Richard's bonus for the first quarter:

- The Practice earns $27,500 for the first quarter, $20,000 above the $7,500 minimum set for this year.

- The Practice has more than $10,000 plus the pool contribution amount in cash on hand.

- At the start of this year, M&B set 45% of the excess as the quarterly contribution to the pool, which for this quarter equals $9,000 (0.45 × $20,000).

- The metrics for Richard are:

  - 100 points for Richard from which 20 points are deducted for each complaint from a client; Richard has 80 points on this metric.

  - 100 points for all his projects being on or under budget, less 10 points for each project over budget; Richard has 90 points on this metric.

  - 100 points for no redesign being required with 1 point deducted for every non-reimbursable $100 of redesign cost to a client; Richard has 80 points on this metric.

  - Richard's total quarterly points thus equal 250.

- His adjustment factor (similar to Zuda's) is 22, which represents the relative importance and influence on profitability that Bob and Mary have assigned to each Project Manager, excluding the impact of Mary and Bob themselves. That's 22 out of 100 for all employees together. Multiplying 250 by 22 gives Bob 5,500 points.

- Everyone else also starts with 300 points, and Richard's figures for the quarter are slightly below the Practice-wide average of 260 points. All of the other employees together have the other 78% (100 – 22), so 78 multiplied by 260 yields 20,280 points. The total points are 20,280 + 5,500 = 25,780, so Richard's percentage of the pool works out to 5,500/25,780 = 21.34%, which yields 21.34% × $9,000 or $1,920.60—somewhat above the $1,800 Richard gave up.

At this rate, Richard gets only another $480 per year, which is not a major improvement for him; but it's important to keep in mind that Richard's performance was *below the average* of all employees. Moreover, the profits the Firm is earning are not robust. If we get to the end of the year with continued improvements incentivized by this system, and Richard is at average points with his cohorts (i.e. 260), and profits have doubled to $55,000, here's what Richard is looking at:

Pool = ($55,000 – $10,000) × 45% = $20,250
Richard's Percentage = (22 × 260)/(78 × 260) + (22 × 260) = 22%
Bonus = $20,250 × 22% = $4,455

That increase in profits is very much the point. If the immediate effect of the bonus system simply increases the Practice's embedded costs without an increase in productivity, efficiency, and profits, the Practice is shooting itself in the foot. Showing Richard and other employees what is possible and achievable is critical to the transition process.

Obviously, the choice of metrics and the entity-wide thresholds are an essential part of the design. Various levels of profit and mixes of performance should be modeled before such a system is finalized and introduced.

Thought also needs to be given to how the pool numbers may change if more employees are added as it's important they not be resented. We'll look at some illustrative possibilities carrying this example forward as we get into the questions of adding another administrator in an upcoming chapter.

## CRACKING THE OVERHEAD NUT

After a brief trip to the water cooler, Mary took a bite out of her granola bar. "Now that we have a great design for fairly compensating our staff," she said to Joseph and Alfred, "how can we better manage overhead costs like this (pointing to the cardboard cup holding her cool, fresh mountain spring water)?!"

Joseph then launched into a series of strategies in response to the overhead question. Some of the solutions applied to direct costs may be similarly applied to reducing overhead. Further, a Practice-wide bonus system that incentivizes care in expenditures ought to produce some savings as individuals are more careful with everything from conserving printer ink to travel expenses. Maybe even some of the same contract terms can produce savings in overhead from vendors.

Still, there is more that can be done.

Again, information is needed to understand where the extra dollars may be. A starting point is to revamp the purchasing system from an *ad hoc* arrangement, perhaps away from frequently and casually used credit cards.

Sloan advised M&B to establish a purchase order log and to use prenumbered purchase orders with preprinted legal terms for all but petty cash items. The legal terms are brief but favorable as shown in Exhibit 4.12.

Whether any circumstance will arise in which these terms will be critical cannot be predicted, but the formality of the document should demand precision in ordering and a touchstone for verifying delivery in case ambiguity in either one has been a cause of some extra costs. Further, the formality removes the ease of picking up the phone or calling up the Internet and providing a credit card number; it requires whoever is doing the ordering to organize their thinking, which should include asking and answering the questions:

■ Is this expense really necessary?

■ Is this the best time to incur the expense?

■ If it's necessary and the time is now, is there a less expensive alternative?

■ Is this an expense that might be billable to a client or otherwise recovered?

The Purchase Order Log is designed to record the following:

■ Purchase order #

**EXHIBIT 4.12** Purchase Order Terms of Transaction

This Purchase Order (P.O.) is not binding upon Buyer until signed by an authorized Buyer representative. All performance and delivery are subject to Buyer approval.

Payment terms are to be calculated from later of delivery or billing date. Only specified charges are allowed. Unless stated otherwise, all payments terms are 2/10, net 30.

Delivery is to be when and where specified, or Buyer may order elsewhere and charge Seller for any extra costs, or Buyer may cancel altogether. Buyer may refuse delivery or tender for Seller error, Seller breach, strike, act of God, other uncontrollable cause or any reason allowed by law. On Buyer demand, Seller shall promptly correct any defects or deviation from Specification.

Seller warrants all goods and services conform to Specifications and all requirements of law, are free of defects, merchantable, fit for Buyer's purposes, and free of encumbrance. Seller further warrants to Buyer all additional warranties required by law and agrees all warranties inure to Buyer's assigns and successors-in-interest of Buyer. Seller warrants all goods delivered and services furnished do not infringe any patent or otherwise violate the right of any person. Seller has full power, authority, and capability to perform according to specifications. Seller warrants insurance coverage for products liability, comprehensive liability, and worker's compensation in commercially reasonable amounts.

As to any Buyer claim, Seller expressly waives all defenses, including without limitation, assumption of risk and contributory negligence. Seller shall reimburse Buyer for all expenses and losses due to any Seller breach.

Unless specified, this P.O. does not include any sales tax collectible from Buyer, which, if applicable are to be separately stated on Seller's invoice. Seller shall be responsible for all other taxes on account of the transaction and shall honor exemption evidence, if presented.

No assignment of this P.O. or change in terms or Specifications is allowed without Buyer's prior written consent. Prior to shipment, Buyer may make written changes to this P.O. Seller's shipment of any part of the order or furnishing of any part of the services constitutes full acceptance of these terms and the entire P.O.

This Agreement is made under and this transaction shall be governed by the laws of the State of Buyer's "bill to" address; the Courts thereof shall have original and sole jurisdiction of any claim arising relative to this transaction. Buyer shall be entitled to recover all costs of suit, including reasonable attorney fees as the prevailing party in any such action.

- Order date

- Person ordering

- Vendor

- Billable to (or "None" if not billable)

- Cost

- Delivery due date.

This information can be captured with a simple database program or even a spreadsheet program. Rearranging the data by delivery due date can help to predict cash outflows, especially if the embedded terms of 2/10 net 30 are retained.

As the database expands, the same kind of analysis can be performed here as was used to analyze the subcontractor overruns. The key variables in this case, however, are likely to be person ordering, vendor, and possibly cost, the latter of which perhaps reflecting less care with smaller orders.

As always, there's no magic wand to overhead control. It requires grinding and continual review as well as efforts to find least cost and to manage vendors with adequate care. However, both Sloan and Wharton underscore the point that the greatest efforts should be made where the greatest dollars are found. Management of purchases requires time and time is costly, so cost–benefit logic should rule here as elsewhere.

## ENSUING DISCUSSION

Sloan stood up, stretched his legs, and walked to the window of the conference room. Looking at the view of the classic New England square, he reflected on the agenda for the next meeting with Bob and Mary. "Cost control is an essential part of good management and critical to preserving profitability. However, no matter how good cost controlling efforts may be, they are not the engine of growth; and without growth, a firm will find itself in a stagnant state at best."

Growth presents its own challenges and risks. We'll look at those critical questions in the following chapter.

# 5

*A business is like a shark; it has to keep moving forward or it dies.*

—paraphrasing *Annie Hall* by Woody Allen[1]

*There are no great limits to growth because there are no limits of human intelligence, imagination, and wonder.*

—Ronald Reagan[2]

# GROWTH AND ITS CONSTRAINTS: MAKING WISE CHOICES

## ORGANISM ANALOGY

An economic unit functions much like an organism. Change one aspect of input and there are both direct and indirect effects that ripple through the

1  Screenplay by Woody Allen and Marshall Brickman, "Annie Hall," in *Four Films of Woody Allen,* New York: Random House, 1982, p. 93.

2  www.quotationspage.com/

organism. Unfortunately, those effects and ripples are not guaranteed to be helpful; they can be harmful.

Like much in life, any change usually carries both some benefits and some disadvantages. The trick is to make choices that are positive. To do that, the decision-maker has to have a pretty accurate idea of how changes impact the economic unit and be able to make a pretty accurate prediction of how those impacts will manifest themselves in financial terms—in the short, intermediate, and long terms.

Prediction is an art, but it can be approached with some scientific tools.

Once predictions are in place, including some calculation of likelihood (also known as risk) it's not too tough to prioritize which changes are most desirable. Then, strategy devolves to tactics to decide on the process to follow to try to make the desired predictions come true.

## WHAT IS GROWTH?

One week later, shortly after 2 p.m., Joseph and Alfred arrived in the parking lot. Each was toting his own briefcase with a laptop stowed safely inside. After Janet had shown them once more to M&B's conference room and made a fresh pot of coffee, the two consultants unpacked, booted up their laptops, and were just connecting the projector when Bob and Mary entered together.

"Mary and I have been discussing the input you've provided to us so far. You know, fellows," Bob related thoughtfully, "we've arrived at the tentative conclusion that if we could just expand our income by about 15 to 20%, I think we'd be in great shape. If there's one thing you could really help us with, that would be it."

"I agree," smiled Mary.

"Interesting observation," Alfred smiled back. "Let me be sure I understand; which income are you two talking about? In fact, I'm wondering if you are both even talking about the same one? Do you mean Practice revenues, Practice profit, Practice cash flow, your individual gross incomes, your individual after-tax incomes, or something else?"

In unison, Bob and Mary responded, "All of them!"

Alfred smiled again. "Okay, which first, or in what order? Because I can assure you they do not magically all come together or, usually, even proximately in time."

Alfred had touched a nerve. The fact is that neither Bob or Mary had really thought through what *growth* might mean. Depending on the answer to Alfred's second question, the routes could be quite different if such growth was achievable at all.

"Let me provide some foundation here," Alfred continued. "Fundamentally, growth in all the bottom line numbers cannot occur unless one of two things or both things happen. Those

**Figure 5.1** Growth has many meanings—and ways to achieve it—depending on specific objectives.

two things, as you well know, are revenues increase and/or costs decrease. That's the simple axiom, but when you start working on all the theorems, lemmas, hypotheses, and corollaries, it's by no means simple." Alfred nodded his head, congratulating himself on his clever geometry metaphor.

"Yes, and here's the first theorem," Joseph said, as he picked up on the metaphor. "*In the long run*, as you intuitively know, you've got to increase revenues while controlling costs to adequately grow. So let's consider *revenue growth* as the tentative definition of what you're seeking. Then we will be able to extrapolate that to other definitions with reasonable time frames."

## THINKING REVENUE

Professional services tend to be purchased least frequently on the basis of fees. The cost is the primary—sometimes the sole—determinant of the purchase of a commodity. As the opposite of a commodity, each professional practice—indeed, each professional—delivers service with uniqueness.

Consequently, underlying any analysis of revenues and plans for increase is the basic truth that a professional must—almost always—be deeply involved in obtaining the purchase commitment from the client. In each contracting effort, if the professional does not measure up to the client's acceptance criteria, no scientific magic is going to increase revenues.

In the final analysis, the professional is, to quote Teddy Roosevelt, "the [wo]man in the ring." However, what consultants (and books) can do is provide guidance to help make the professional's presentation and appearance to the client as strong as possible, in part by helping to choose the prospective clients on whom effort should be expended in the first place.

## BASELINE REVENUE ANALYSIS

Recall, please, from Chapter 3 that M&B's greatest direct profit was coming from commercial work for commercial clients. Deeper analysis is in order to verify that there is not some outlier or other artifact in each line of business that is creating a false impression.

Revenues can be examined from several perspectives to see where increase(s) may be driven and further refined within those perspectives. The main perspectives for a professional practice are projects, output, and fee. The way those three perspectives can be cross-sectioned is by type of service, number of clients, and type of client. So first, M&B has made the data available for Sloan and Wharton to calculate some averages, by month, quarter, and year:

- Average Revenue per Client (ARC);

- Average Revenue per Project (ARP);

- Average Fee per Billable Professional Hour (APH).[3]

Sloan and Wharton want to first make calculations for the Practice as a whole in order to see how it is doing in relation to the market at large. Then they can drill down deeper into that information to see how those baseline numbers work out by project type or division of revenue.

The number of clients, projects, and professionals' hours billed, are (luckily and wisely) all tracked on a monthly basis by the Firm, so the consultants are able to calculate those key averages with the data supplied by the Firm. First, they want to determine the number of clients and the number of projects that were active in each month and quarter throughout the year from that date. Exhibit 5.1 shows those base numbers.

---

3   For simplicity's sake, we've defined M&B as having no billable nonprofessionals; but if a practice does have such nonprofessionals then an additional statistic would be calculated: *Average Fee per All Billable Hours (APB)*.

**EXHIBIT 5.1** Client and Engagement Annual Totals

| 20XX | Clients | | | | | Projects | | | | |
|---|---|---|---|---|---|---|---|---|---|---|
| | **Open** | **End** | **Add** | **Open+Add** | **Close** | **Open** | **End** | **Add** | **Open+Add** | **Close** |
| Jan. | 11 | 1 | 0 | 11 | 10 | 14 | 1 | 0 | 14 | 13 |
| Feb. | 10 | 1 | 3 | 13 | 12 | 13 | 1 | 1 | 14 | 13 |
| Mar. | 12 | 0 | 2 | 14 | 14 | 13 | 0 | 1 | 14 | 14 |
| Qtr1 | | | | 16 | | | | | 16 | |
| Apr. | 14 | 0 | 0 | 14 | 14 | 14 | 0 | 1 | 15 | 15 |
| May | 14 | 0 | 1 | 15 | 15 | 15 | 0 | 1 | 16 | 16 |
| Jun. | 15 | 1 | 1 | 16 | 15 | 16 | 1 | 2 | 18 | 17 |
| Qtr2 | | | | 16 | | | | | 18 | |
| Jul. | 15 | 2 | 0 | 15 | 13 | 17 | 2 | 2 | 19 | 17 |
| Aug. | 13 | 1 | 2 | 15 | 14 | 17 | 1 | 0 | 17 | 16 |
| Sep. | 14 | 0 | 2 | 16 | 16 | 16 | 2 | 2 | 18 | 16 |
| Qtr3 | | | | 19 | | | | | 21 | |
| Oct. | 16 | 1 | 1 | 17 | 16 | 16 | 1 | 3 | 19 | 18 |
| Nov. | 16 | 2 | 0 | 16 | 14 | 18 | 2 | 2 | 20 | 18 |
| Dec. | 14 | 0 | 0 | 14 | 14 | 18 | 2 | 0 | 18 | 16 |
| Qtr4 | | | | 17 | | | | | 21 | |
| | | | | | | | | | | |
| SUMS | | 9 | 12 | | | | 13 | 15 | | |
| TOTALS | OPEN + ADDS: **23*** | | | | | OPEN + ADDS: **29*** | | | | |

Note: *The totals start with the January open figure and add the additional projects obtained during the year. Projects ending are still worked on during the year. The number of active clients and active projects each month and quarter are also potentially useful statistics to have available.

Similarly, the totals by quarter for the number of clients and number of projects are again not just arithmetic sums of what's in a column. The total number of clients for whom work was performed and the total number of projects on which work was performed in any period is equal to the opening number for the first month of the quarter plus all those added clients or projects during that quarter. Any that dropped off during the quarter still had work done during the period if they were active at the quarter's start (i.e. included in the opening balance), so they still count as active during the quarter for the purposes of the averages.

Further, of course, it is not tautological that the number of clients will always equal the number of projects. In fact for M&B, there are several clients who have more than one project in process at any one time. Consequently, the completion of a project does not necessarily mean that the client is still not counted if one or more projects of that client are still in process.

Now, with Exhibit 5.1's calculations in place, Sloan and Wharton can calculate Practice-wide averages in Exhibit 5.2, as follows.

**EXHIBIT 5.2** Practice-Wide Averages

| | REVENUE AVERAGES FOR YEAR 20XX | | | | | | AVERAGES | | | |
|---|---|---|---|---|---|---|---|---|---|---|
| 20XX | Revenue ($) | – Sub Fees ($) | Adj. Rev. ($) | Clients | ARC ($) | Projects | ARP ($) | Hours | AFH ($) |
| Jan. | 103,168 | 15,743 | 87,425 | 11 | 7,948 | 14 | 6,245 | 956 | 91 |
| Feb. | 99,654 | 34,596 | 65,058 | 13 | 5,004 | 13 | 5,004 | 930 | 70 |
| Mar. | 131,568 | 32,910 | 98,658 | 14 | 7,047 | 14 | 7,047 | 1,023 | 96 |
| Qtr1 | 334,390 | 83,249 | 251,141 | 16 | 15,696 | 16 | 15,696 | 2,937 | 86 |
| Apr. | 135,193 | 33,000 | 102,193 | 14 | 7,300 | 15 | 6,813 | 1,084 | 94 |
| May | 125,055 | 37,898 | 87,157 | 15 | 5,810 | 16 | 5,447 | 1,085 | 80 |
| Jun. | 158,544 | 30,384 | 128,160 | 16 | 8,010 | 17 | 7,539 | 1,190 | 108 |
| Qtr2 | 418,792 | 101,283 | 317,510 | 16 | 19,844 | 18 | 17,639 | 3,359 | 95 |
| Jul. | 143,344 | 30,188 | 113,156 | 15 | 7,544 | 17 | 6,656 | 1,133 | 100 |
| Aug. | 118,799 | 19,932 | 98,867 | 16 | 6,179 | 16 | 6,179 | 1,116 | 89 |
| Sep. | 134,023 | 22,154 | 111,869 | 17 | 6,581 | 16 | 6,992 | 1,121 | 100 |
| Qtr3 | 396,166 | 72,274 | 323,892 | 19 | 17,047 | 21 | 15,423 | 3,390 | 96 |
| Oct. | 144,620 | 25,925 | 118,695 | 17 | 6,982 | 18 | 6,594 | 1,071 | 111 |
| Nov. | 136,319 | 17,743 | 118,576 | 16 | 7,411 | 18 | 6,588 | 1,094 | 108 |
| Dec. | 115,854 | 22,926 | 92,928 | 14 | 6,638 | 16 | 5,808 | 1,024 | 91 |
| Qtr4 | 396,793 | 66,594 | 330,199 | 17 | 19,423 | 21 | 15,724 | 3,220 | 103 |
| Year | 1,546,141 | 323,400 | 1,222,741 | 23 | 53,163 | 29 | 42,163 | 12,906 | 94.74 |
| Avg/Mo. | 128,845 | 26,950 | 101,895 | 15 | 6,869 | 16 | 6,435 | 1,069 | 95.33 |
| Avg/Qtr. | 386,535 | 80,850 | 305,685 | 17 | 17,981 | 19 | 16,089 | 3,227 | 94.74 |

**Key:**

ARC = Average Revenue per Client
ARP = Average Revenue per Project
AFH = Average Fee per Professional Hour

Before analyzing what Exhibit 5.2 discloses, the consultants first compare apples with apples by adjusting for the subcontractor fees charged to clients by the Firm, which include a 10% standard markup on all subcontractor charges. That's why the second numerical column is shown as "– Sub Fees". Once that adjusting subtraction is made for each period (again using data from M&B's internal accounting records), what's left for analysis are the revenues produced by the work of the Practice's employees. That adjustment calculation is shown in the first three numerical columns.

The number of clients and the number of projects are derived from Exhibit 5.1 to calculate those averages, and the professional hours are available from the billing records, so all the input is there for the averages to be calculated. (In contrast to clients and projects, the quarterly and yearly figures for professional hours are indeed straightforward additions.)

Now, what do Sloan and Wharton see? Wharton began: "Just from the methodology, I have to note that with the industry standard of only 10% in markup for subcontractors, if any of that work can be lawfully (i.e. by licensure) performed within the Firm and be billable then you're giving away gross profit when you use any subcontractor for that work, assuming the work can be efficiently performed in-house. The logical next question is can you do the work? And if the answer is no, should you be thinking about adding a professional who can? Perhaps an in-house structural engineer? We'll come back to that later, but I wanted to get it out on the table."

Wharton continued: "Anyway, looking at these numbers, your job size isn't too bad and you are earning a decent average amount from each job per month, but the turnover is interesting. What I mean by that word, *turnover*, is that your monthly revenue average is exceeding your quarterly average and that's exceeding the annual average. Here's why I say that," and he showed the calculation in Exhibit 5.3.

**EXHIBIT 5.3** Project Turnover Impacts on Revenue

|  | Average ($) | Multiple | Extrapolated ($) | Yearly ($) | Year Shortfall ($) |
| --- | --- | --- | --- | --- | --- |
| Month | 6,869 | 12 | 82,432 | 53,163 | 29,269 |
| Quarter | 17,981 | 4 | 71,926 | 53,163 | 18,763 |

"These shortfalls *may* be an artifact because your activity is trending up, but what it may also indicate is that your work is highly front-loaded with more hours and billing going on in the early part of a project when you are getting familiar with it and that winding down as you move along. That's not necessarily bad, but if you are giving clients fixed fee or capped proposals then that could be dangerous because it suggests the possibility that you may be shaving hours from your invoices or you may not be putting in adequate effort as you get near the end of a project. I've seen situations where the project manager may do that without the knowledge of a firm's principals. Here's some further analysis that suggests this may be happening. Maybe not across the board, but perhaps sometimes."

Wharton paired monthly hours worked from Exhibit 5.2, first with new project starts and then with project terminations, both from Exhibit 5.1. First though, he calculated a variance against the average of hours worked in each month.

Wharton spoke softly as he made his point: "The correlation coefficients of the two pairings were each positive, suggesting there is some relationship between hours worked and the turnover in projects. The correlation to terminations (0.171), however, was very weak, suggesting that winding down a project didn't make too great a difference. Yet, the initiation

**EXHIBIT 5.4** Project Turnover Impact

| 20XX | Hours | Variance | Add | End |
|---|---|---|---|---|
| Jan. | 956 | −113 | 0 | 1 |
| Feb. | 930 | −139 | 1 | 1 |
| Mar. | 1,023 | −46 | 1 | 0 |
| Apr. | 1,084 | 15 | 1 | 0 |
| May | 1,085 | 16 | 1 | 0 |
| Jun. | 1,190 | 121 | 2 | 1 |
| Jul. | 1,133 | 64 | 2 | 2 |
| Aug. | 1,116 | 47 | 0 | 1 |
| Sep. | 1,121 | 52 | 2 | 2 |
| Oct. | 1,071 | 2 | 3 | 1 |
| Nov. | 1,094 | 25 | 2 | 2 |
| Dec. | 1,024 | −45 | 0 | 2 |
| Average | 1,069 | 0 | | |
| Coeff. Correl. | | | 0.47712782 | 0.17102827 |

of new projects showed a stronger, though not robust, correlation of 0.477. Do you think recorded time shaving is occurring?"

Bob and Mary glanced at each other.

Mary answered first: "With some of these clients, I think it's a fact of life. We pride ourselves on service and that means making the client happy. In this market and this economy, we are not in a position to hammer clients on every dime."

Bob said, "Yeah, I guess it's possible; I don't know."

Mary replied: "Come on, Bob. I think what Alfred is saying is we can't let it become a habit."

Alfred smiled. "That's right, Mary. What this data suggests to me is that this issue, if it's real, may arise intermittently or, more troublingly, may be due to one person who is managing projects. Or it could be due to the kind of project that is starting. We could develop more statistics and they may or may not correlate in some way, but correlation is not real proof; it can be coincidental. You may have heard, for example, that if the NFC team wins the Super Bowl in any year, correlation statistics say the stock market as measured by the Dow ends up higher for that year.[4] There are some theories about why there may be a connection, but *come on! Really!?!* You get my point.

---

4   See www.snopes.com/business/bank/superbowl.asp, among others.

"Better than more numbers, I suggest that you two," motioning to Bob and Mary, "just talk with your Project Managers and see what they have to say. Don't make it an accusation; it's a question. If it's happening, there may be good reasons, and in any event, your managers are trying to do the right thing and not upset or lose clients. I think, Mary, your answer shows you recognize that.

"But you need to know because . . . I'll call it a syndrome . . . because that syndrome needs to be taken into account in your fee development and because there are probably better ways to handle the issue, at least sometimes, in terms of time and personnel management. And again, timely and well-communicated information on what's happening is your first line of defense."

It was Joseph's turn: "Some other observations arising from Exhibit 5.2:

1. Once the subcontractor fees are out of the mix, we see you increased your in-house-generated revenue every quarter. That's a plus.

2. It's especially a plus because it's readily apparent that active clients and active projects were trending up right along with revenues. That shows the growth is real.

3. One piece of bad news is that your average project appears to be pretty small in terms of revenue. A silver lining is that you are not overly dependent on one client or a couple of big jobs, but it does mean you don't get a good opportunity for economies of scale. It also suggests there's a greater likelihood that you as owners, without great management depth, will be pulled in many directions at once. That can be pretty wearing and distracting. It works against additional profitable growth.

4. Those small numbers may also indicate you are leaving some money on the table when you send out quotes and proposals. In other words, your fees based on time may be too low.

5. And that indication seems to be validated by the somewhat anemic rate you are earning compared to the market on professional hours. Our research suggests that in this market, you should have an average rate for your mix of personnel of between $120 and $125 per hour. You are substantially under that—by roughly 20%—at $95; just $94.74[5] to be exact. This last point is particularly striking, and I think you can see why we consider it to be such an important finding. If you can raise rates and hold your project volume, pretty much all of that increase can flow right to the bottom line.

6. As stated, your volume of clients and projects are both increasing, but there's a cautionary question: Are those increases occurring simply because your rates are low? From our discussions with you, we know that you are not interested in selling a commodity, that the passion for both of you is to produce great designs—both aesthetically and functionally."

---

5   The monthly figure is slightly different due to rounding effects. The annual figure presents the most reliable as it's a single calculation incorporating all data reviewed for the year.

Mary and Bob both nodded appreciatively. Then Bob said: "You know what's interesting is that the government work, which we've spent so much time discussing, is always so competitive that we feel our rates are being depressed in that segment. But we look at it as worth the effort. For one thing, we like the public service aspect. For another, we think the fact we get that imprimatur gives people confidence, especially for residential. And then lastly, the nature of the work lets us do some useful training for our interns. Do you think that the government work is skewing the numbers?"

Joseph replied: "Well, we looked at that. Here's what we saw when we drilled down among those three revenue divisions."

**EXHIBIT 5.5** Revenue Averages as a Function of Project Type

| 20XX | Adj. Rev. ($) | Clients | ARC ($) | Projects | ARP ($) | Hours | APH ($) |
|------|---------------|---------|---------|----------|---------|-------|---------|
| | | | REVENUE AVERAGES FOR YEAR 20XX | | | | |
| Residential | 519,354 | 9 | 57,706 | 13 | 39,950 | 5,334 | **97.37** |
| Commercial | 604,063 | 11 | 54,915 | 12 | 50,339 | 5,848 | **103.29** |
| Government | 98,995 | 3 | 32,998 | 4 | 24,749 | 1,724 | **57.42** |
| **ALL M&B** | **1,222,741** | **23** | **53,163** | **29** | **42,163** | **12,906** | **94.74** |

Leaning forward, Alfred took over the discussion. "As you can see, the government work does skew the numbers, but that $94.74 figure is a *weighted* average. Since the government work is a relatively small proportion of the total, the impact is not so great though it's definitely an area of concern. The average between residential and commercial is just about $100 per hour; so at $57.42 for government, it's basically 43% below the others. If I was in your shoes, Bob, I'm not sure I'd feel that enormous differential is justified. But whether it is or isn't, the fact is all three divisions are materially below the market averages."

"Where that takes us," Joseph interjected, "is that the analysis necessarily tends to become more subjective at this point in trying to pinpoint the cause or causes. We wondered if maybe there was a programming flaw in your proposal templates, but that checked out. So if proposal development is the cause, it's a function of the inputs being estimated. Another possibility is that your billing is not picking up all the charges. We've talked about that a bit on the government work and you've confirmed that is happening, but it's hard to imagine that's the whole cause. In all likelihood, there is not a single cause.

"Let me cut to the chase. Alfred and I think this problem relates directly to the question of whether M&B should hire a business development/marketing specialist. Here's how we see it . . .

"Assume you just stay even in the coming year with the same number of projects: 23. And assume too that you hold the same mix of projects among those three revenue divisions and that the level of effort to complete those jobs will be roughly the same.

"*But*, now assume that the number one priority you assign to the specialist is to help you bring in this work at a minimum average of $115 per professional's hour for commercial and residential projects and $75 per hour for government work. Those are increased rates but still below the market averages range. If you can do that, here's the marginal revenue that M&B will gain from that work, *provided* you keep the same mix of revenue among those three divisions."

**EXHIBIT 5.6** Revenue at Target Minimum Fees

|  | Hours | Target/Hr. | Revenue | AFH |
|---|---|---|---|---|
| Residential ($) | 5,334 | 115 | 613,410 |  |
| Commercial ($) | 5,848 | 115 | 672,520 |  |
| Government ($) | 1,724 | 75 | 129,300 |  |
| ALL M&B ($) | 12,906 |  | 1,415,230 | **110** |
| Less: 20XX Adj. Revenue ($) |  |  | 1,222,741 | 95 |
| Marginal Revenue Added ($) |  |  | **192,489** | 15 |
| Percentage Increase |  |  | 15.74 | 15.43 |

"Now, we posit that the question to resolve is framed this way: 'Can you find a specialist who can help you accomplish this feat at a cost less than $192,489?' And if the answer is yes, can the specialist and the Firm expand its overall revenues further from there?

"Take note that a fee increase constitutes an unusual, indeed a unique, opportunity because we are postulating that other than the costs attendant to the specialist—salary, payroll overhead, auto expenses, etc.—the increase is all pretax profit. In contrast, for just about every kind of improvement in operations, we'd all be necessarily focusing on and measuring the benefit in terms of the incremental addition of gross profit from the revenue increase, not the revenue itself. In other words, the marginal benefits are only those that would exist *after* deducting the costs that must be expended in order to produce that marginal revenue.

"Not here! That's the magic of fee increases—they don't generate costs.

"But as always in the dismal science of economics, there's no free lunch. What fee increases may portend, as you well know, is the risk that demand for your services may decline, taking with it some of that anticipated revenue—or more. That's part of the specialist's job—to evaluate that risk and to market accordingly to protect against that downside.

"Hence, our suggestion is tentative and no automatic panacea; it deserves study and reflection by you as the experts on your Firm, your clientele, and your market. Can the market absorb this ratchet upward? Will your existing clients accept it? Will you still have the needed market power and competitive advantage to secure those projects and their concomitant revenues in the face of fee resistance? If you think you can, then this concept would seem to work." (See Chapter 7 for an analysis on how to justify increased fees.)

"We also believe that if you hire the right specialist, there may be ancillary benefits, particularly in time savings for both of you and the corresponding benefits from your increased availability to exercise managerial oversight. For example, perhaps such assistance will free each of you to a degree that will allow you to ferret out and control that insidious cost creep. Or by taking some of the marketing burden from the professional staff, it will allow them to pick up some of the work with a healthier gross margin that is currently being performed by your subcontractors at a mere 10% markup. Further, to the extent it allows you to replace administrative hours with billable hours, that's another possible ancillary benefit. If that occurs, you can look at those revenues as increasing the affordability of the specialist.

"Nevertheless, while we're pretty confident ancillary benefits will arise, we don't want to count on those plusses to justify the decision. The more so because those ancillary plusses are difficult and speculative to predict, so we recommend that the point on which the decision should rise or fall is the objective metric of a specific target minimum for average hourly fees.

"Two other points to consider in weighing this proposition:

1. It may be that rather than hiring an employee, for the same or less money you might subcontract the effort to a firm that specializes in such marketing efforts. That's another aspect to investigate. One potential advantage to that approach is that you might be able to negotiate a contract that varies to the extent the consultant meets the goals.

2. To be realistic, we cannot expect that you'll flip a switch and overnight you will see fees and fee income increase by over 15%. For one thing, you're already pretty much locked in to completing your backlog at the contracted fees. That means there will be a period of investment and the investment must be recouped. Milestones and a deadline are essential, as well as a monitoring plan."

## THE EFFICIENCY QUESTION

Wharton and Sloan were not finished yet. Alfred brought another spreadsheet to the screen and said: "There's one other set of statistics that come out of this part of our analysis, and it is as important as any other we've discussed because it has some important implications." He asked Bob and Mary to look at Exhibit 5.7.

"Exhibit 5.7 looks strictly at hours. There are eight professionals in the Firm and they are the ones generating fees by working these hours. The table is derived from the information that was developed for Exhibit 5.3. The concept is quite simple:

▪ Column 1 is taken right from Exhibit 5.3; the total hours billed by the professionals.

▪ Column 2 divides Column 1 by the number of professionals, i.e. eight, which produces the average number of hours each has billed in each month (or quarter) over the course of the year.

**EXHIBIT 5.7** Billing Efficiencies and Utilization Rates

| 20XX | Average Professional Hours/Week: 47.5 | | | |
| | Column | | | |
| | 1 | 2 | 3 | 4 |
| | #Prof. Hrs. | Per Emp. | Emp/Wk | Utilization % |
|---|---|---|---|---|
| Jan. | 956 | 120 | 27.47 | 57.83 |
| Feb. | 930 | 116 | 26.72 | 56.26 |
| Mar. | 1,023 | 128 | 29.40 | 61.89 |
| *Qtr1* | *2,937* | *367* | *28.15* | *59.27* |
| Apr. | 1,084 | 136 | 31.15 | 65.58 |
| May | 1,085 | 136 | 31.18 | 65.64 |
| Jun. | 1,190 | 149 | 34.20 | 71.99 |
| *Qtr2* | *3,359* | *420* | *32.20* | *67.79* |
| Jul. | 1,133 | 142 | 32.56 | 68.54 |
| Aug. | 1,116 | 140 | 32.07 | 67.51 |
| Sep. | 1,121 | 140 | 32.21 | 67.82 |
| *Qtr3* | *3,390* | *424* | *32.50* | *68.41* |
| Oct. | 1,071 | 134 | 30.78 | 64.79 |
| Nov. | 1,094 | 137 | 31.44 | 66.18 |
| Dec. | 1,024 | 128 | 29.43 | 61.95 |
| *Qtr4* | *3,220* | *403* | *30.87* | *64.98* |
| | | | | |
| Avg./Mo. | 1,069 | 134 | 30.72 | 64.67 |
| | | | | |
| Avg./Qtr. | 3,227 | 403 | 30.72 | 64.67 |
| | | | | |
| Year | 12,906 | 1,613 | 30.72 | 64.67 |

- Column 3 then divides those monthly hours by 4.29 (the number of weeks in an average month)[6] or for the quarters (by averaging its 3 months), in all cases to calculate the number of hours billed per week, on average, by each of the professionals. The year equals the average for all the months.[7]

- Column 4 divides those average weeks by the average hours worked by each of the professionals. We calculated, after interviewing the staff, that including some time worked

---

6  Average Month = 30 days; 7 days per week; 30/7 = 4.29 weeks per average month.
7  Of course, because the quarter and year figures are averages of the preceding average, they're all equal. If 13.04 weeks per quarter or 52.14 weeks per year were used, the results would vary by a few percentage points.

evenings and weekends, the average is 47.5 hours per week. The result then in the fourth column of Exhibit 5.7 is the average percentage of those average 47.5 hours of work time that is billed, i.e. that produces revenue for the Firm (subject to collection). This statistic is a *Utilization Rate*. It's a measure of staff efficiency.

"You know you can't bill 100% of your time. Over the course of the year, administrative activities, vacations, sick time, training, marketing, client relations, etc. all steal time from the billable pool. In fact, I'm sure you'll agree that there's rarely a day when anyone can just bill 100% of their work time for that day. It's the nature of the beast, that beast being the time clock to which we are all slaves.

"Even when working on fixed fee projects, there is a practical time budget limitation to make the fee worthwhile, which is translatable into an hourly rate. Effectively, those hours worked on a fixed fee contract are billable because the fees are not earned until each milestone is reached at which point the revenues belong to the Firm.

"Experience and research show that for design professionals, it is very difficult—even unusual—to exceed 75%[8] in billable hours. Even 70% is a rather significant achievement. In fact, for engineering firms, a significant portion of your consultants, the more common anecdotal standard may be as low as 67%[9]—just two-thirds of the time.

"Your Utilization Rate is coming in at 64.67%. That's pretty darn high. The good news is that it says your staff is focused and probably doing a pretty good job of timekeeping. The not so good news is that 64.67% suggests that M&B is nearing the practical limit of its capacity.

"That, in turn, raises some difficult questions for you:

- How much additional revenue can be earned with present professional staffing?

- At what point is it wise to add professional staff?

- What will it cost to add professional staff?

- How will additions to staff be funded?

Let's take those questions in order" (see below).

## POTENTIAL REVENUE

Alfred's first question now popped up on the screen: *How much additional revenue can be earned with present professional staffing?*

---

8  See, for example, http://glossary.tenrox.com/Utililization-Rate.htm
9  id.

"Speaking simplistically, if you're at 64.67% and that's producing $1,222,741 in revenue (exclusive of subcontractor or consultant revenue) then all we have to do is extrapolate to 75% maximum utilization to see the theoretical limit":

$(75.00\%/64.67\%) \times \$1,222,741 = \$1,418,054$
$\$1,418,054 - \$1,222,741 = \$195,313$
$\$195,313/\$1,222,741 = 16\%$ increase

"Now, here's something interesting," Alfred was actually grinning and he winked at Joseph. "Your intuitions seem right on track. I say that because at the start of our meeting today, you both focused on increasing income '15 to 20%' and 16% falls right into that range. The point at which an economic enterprise is theoretically going to have its greatest profit is when it is at its rated capacity. It may be able to increase output beyond that capacity, but just like a machine that runs above its rated capacity, dysfunctions and blips start to show up and it cannot run for any substantial duration at that rate without risking some kind of failure. If the demand for such overload output continues, the enterprise has to increase capacity. You both sensed that 16% more is that rated capacity. That shows you are in touch. But I'm also sure you would not be content to achieve that goal and then just sit on that plateau indefinitely—even if the market would let you do so. We have to think growth and we are here to help you do so strategically."

Joseph brought the conversation back to focus on where these numbers were leading. "Remember though, it's not the billable hours worked that we are looking at here but the billable hours as recorded in your database. So there's a chance that utilization is higher and the 16% cushion is actually smaller.

"On the other side of the coin, perhaps there are steps that might be taken to yield more revenue with the current staff:

- Increasing fee rates, as we've already discussed, but note that such increases aren't producing real growth in the Firm's place in the market but, rather, are only extracting more from that static place. That's not to demean fee increases if they can be competitively successful; the point is that fee increases are an interim tactic, not a growth strategy.

- Maybe a few extra hours can be added to that average, perhaps getting as high as 50, but that's *really* pushing it.

- Switching to fixed fee work or including some mix of fixed fee work might capture some marginal revenues. That would be the case if clients agree to a fee that ends up yielding more than the hourly charges would amount to, either because you successfully sell the sizzle or the work is accomplished with greater efficiency than what's budgeted. In a sense, it can be a way to institute fee increases without saying so. Nevertheless, practically speaking, fixed fees are a gamble that introduces a material measure of risk. Frankly, our research in this region says that fixed fee work is somewhat of an unusual market practice, which makes it even more risky from a client relations standpoint. (See Chapter 7 for a discussion on smart fees.)

- Reorganizing work might allow you to somehow exceed 75% but rare is the firm that can sustain that degree of efficiency for any extended period of time, especially if you experience some turnover in staff, which is inevitable, not to mention the black swans of disruption.

"On that last point, we should emphasize that 75% is considered an *ideal*; your true limit may be lower. Remember that 67% figure for engineers? That's probably the number at which strain begins to manifest itself. If that turns out to be the best M&B can do, which, don't get me wrong, is still a pretty admirable rate, the limit becomes:

$$(67\%/64.67\%) \times \$1,222,741 = \$1,266,795$$
$$\$1,266,795 - \$1,222,741 = \$44,054$$
$$\$44,054/\$1,222,741 = 3.6\% \text{ increase}$$

"The sum of $44k is just about equal to one more average project's revenue over the course of the year,[10] so as a practical matter, you might possibly be at the limit already."

Mary knitted her brow. "I wonder," she said, "could that be one of the reasons underlying our frustrations? We need more staff? It's easy to add the expense, but that doesn't automatically produce the income. We've got to add clients and projects too. With right-sized fees to match!"

Bob nodded vigorously in agreement and added: "We're straining with our cash flow now. I've been able to follow everything else you've said, but this sounds counterintuitive! The staff has to come *after* we have more work, not *before. Right?!?*"

"Right," Alfred quickly rejoined, "But there's a problem—really a multifaceted problem—to address. Think of it this way: if you just grow with the same operating profile as you have now, your finances don't really improve. Your profits, indeed your salaries, are unsatisfactory. Multiplying those current figures by some degree of revenue increase will only yield the same anemic returns and unsatisfactory results. So what we're driving at is a *strategic plan*, which is more than bouncing from tactic to tactic until the next crisis erupts that demands another palliative tactic. You're absolutely right about the cash flow; and you can even add that increasing staff, even by just one person, has implications for overhead increases—everything from supplies used to telephone costs, furniture, and computer equipment. We want to take you through the answers to those other three tactical questions: when to add, what the costs are, and how to fund those costs. We want to do that and more, but our responses will be in the context of promoting the strategic goals we set forth at the start, which can be shorthanded as *growth with more income*."

Joseph jumped in at this point. "We're saying it's multifaceted because capacity is a facet, raising fee rates is a facet, marketing, time allocations, cost control—all are other facets. The tactics address those but they need to be coordinated so that a solution here does not beget

---

10   See Exhibit 5.2.

new problems there or intensify old problems somewhere else. So let me mention another tactic to consider while we're at it.

"Remember earlier in this conversation today, we talked about profits you might be 'giving away' to consultants if you could handle that work yourself. Part of what's disclosed by this analysis is that adding the right kind of person might not require you to go through a major marketing effort if you can fund that new person to an adequate extent by examining potential projects from conception for more of the contract revenue anticipated instead of readily turning that work over to consultants. Perhaps, it may even be possible to mine some existing projects as change orders arise or if consultants drop out for any reason. At the same time, that added person could also be your safety valve for a while to increase your overall capacity. That's not the whole story, but it is another corollary."

After a pause while Bob and Mary made some notes, Alfred spoke: "The hour is late. I think we ought to knock off for the day and pick up tomorrow. That'll give you a chance to digest what we've gotten through so far, the vast majority of which, in one way or another, enters into a synthesis for producing the strategic planning we want to leave you with. Note, that I didn't say 'strategic plan'—that's a static view; I said '*planning*.' We want to leave you with a dynamic model that you can revisit and reuse as changes and developments occur."

Joseph nodded. Mary and Bob both smiled back.

"Okay," said Alfred, closing his laptop and disconnecting from the projector. "Thanks for letting us avoid the worst of rush hour. We'll see you tomorrow at 10 a.m. to elaborate on the issues we raised today and have a conversation about strategic financial planning."

**6**

# STRATEGIC FINANCIAL PLANNING: SETTING AND REACHING PROFIT TARGETS

## CONUNDRUM: PEOPLE AND CAPITAL

At 10:03 a.m. on an overcast Friday morning, Mary Michelangelo stared with fixed gaze into her coffee cup, intently stirring its contents, as if scrutinizing a fortune teller's tea leaves for answers, her mouth set in a near grimace. "You

1   www.quotationspage.com/
2   www.quotationspage.com/

know," she said, addressing Sloan and Wharton, "I feel as though what we've discussed so far is like the sugar I just dissolved into this cup of coffee. Your recommendations will make this a little sweeter, but the real substance of what we've got is still pretty much the same. I mean, the tactics are helpful—they are—but I don't see us being able to seize the brass ring. We don't have enough people and we don't have enough capital. If we bring in those receivables and save a bunch of those costs, yes, they right the ship, but it seems to me we're still under sail in an age of steam."

"Those are great metaphors, Mary," Joseph replied, "and I think you are focused on the foundational conundrum—people and capital—but I think in today's meeting, to borrow your metaphor, we can provide you with the final tools to retrofit your schooner with the engine that will allow Michelangelo & Brunelleschi to proceed 'full steam ahead.'"

Sloan continued: "To this point, most everything we've talked about has been internal to your firm, but one issue we want to address today is the broad view of externalities. One externality is the market in which you compete. Another is the state of the economy in which that market exists. Having a sense of where the economy and your market are headed is one tool for unraveling that conundrum.

"Another tool will let you model those different tactics—those 'sweeteners' as you refer to them—to test whether they are giving you the desired results you are seeking. This second tool will permit you to test in advance to see if the sugar, cream, and cinnamon have been added in the right proportions to your coffee and to see if the coffee itself is served at the right temperature. So you see, Mary, we're going to do more than just alter the taste. We want to establish a regimen for you that will help you be satisfied, indeed pleased, with the drink."

Mary smiled at the way her metaphor had been expanded. "I can't wait to start using those," she said.

Joe and Alfred both smiled back.

## LOOKING OUTWARD

Alfred had turned on his laptop and fired up the conference room projector once again during the exchange between Mary and Joseph. Alfred nodded to Joseph to signal his readiness. Bob grinned at their coordination and wondered how many times they had made presentations like this one. Bob realized their gray hair signaled this was definitely not their first rodeo.

Alfred was indeed ready: "You've been in your own Practice now for 11 years. Like many folks who break out on their own, you chose to do so at a point when the economy was pretty strong, so you got a leg up on establishing yourselves. At this point, 11 years later, you've been through a downturn; we're all seeing the economy and the local market making something of a comeback, but the statistics show the economy is still not robust, especially in this part of the country, which was hit hard by some of the losses in manufacturing during the downturn. Maybe that's been a factor for some of those slow-pay receivables.

**EXHIBIT 6.1** Economic and Market Correlations

| Year | M&B Revenues ($) | U.S. Gross Domestic Product (GDP) ($ trillion) | Regional New Permits (No.) | Year-End Unemployment (%) |
|------|------|------|------|------|
| 0 | 0 | 11,510.7 | 10,204 | 5.7 |
| 1 | 387,992 | 12,274.9 | 11,454 | 5.4 |
| 2 | 623,054 | 13,093.7 | 12,524 | 4.9 |
| 3 | 783,944 | 13,855.9 | 11,135 | 4.4 |
| 4 | 1,010,209 | 14,477.6 | 8,257 | 5.0 |
| 5 | 1,005,062 | 14,718.6 | 5,372 | 7.3 |
| 6 | 844,754 | 14,418.7 | 3,568 | 9.9 |
| 7 | 915,488 | 14,964.4 | 3,568 | 9.3 |
| 8 | 1,027,434 | 15,517.9 | 3,858 | 8.5 |
| 9 | 1,145,683 | 16,163.2 | 5,146 | 7.9 |
| 10 | 1,322,097 | 16,768.1 | 5,919 | 6.7 |
| 11 | 1,546,541 | 17,420.7 | 6,108 | 5.6 |
| 11-Year Correlation* | | 97.69% | −57.58% | 15.00% |
| 5-Year Correlation** | | | 96.78% | −99.61% |

Notes: Except for the most recent year, all of the other revenue figures are introduced here for the first time, coming from M&B's financial statement archives.

* Revenues correlated within the same year to each of the three statistics.

** Most recent 5 years of Revenues correlated to the immediately preceding year's figure for Regional New Permits and Year-End Unemployment; e.g. Years 6–11 Revenues matched to Years 5–10 Regional New Permits.

"With that as background, I think you'll find the numbers we ran, which are up on the screen (Exhibit 6.1), to be rather interesting.

"What you see in Exhibit 6.1 is a comparison of M&B revenues throughout your 11-year history to three economic statistics that we identified in a search for correlative numbers. Those three statistics are:

- U.S. Gross Domestic Product, which is the sum of all economic activity in the nation throughout the year; but this is the so-called *Current* Dollar figure, meaning there is no adjustment for inflation.

- Regional New Housing Unit Permits in Number of Units in your region, one of four for the country. That's all kinds of units, single family and multifamily, in all categories.

- The National Unemployment Rate as a percentage of the workforce. This is the most commonly quoted unemployment rate—even though it only is based on people defined as looking for work and ignores various segments of the working-age population who by U.S. Labor Department sampling are not in the workforce, so the real rate tends to be higher.

"Correlation of the first two columns shows a very strong match, indicating that over the 11 years of existence, M&B's revenues have closely tracked the Gross Domestic Product—the primary measure of economic activity for the United States. On a current basis, if economic activity is down, M&B can expect their revenues to be down too. Likewise on the upside, the two would also be expected to be on parallel tracks.

"Keep in mind, please, that's useful information, but not terribly useful for the purpose of forecasting because by the time the economic statistics are available, the results for M&B will likely be on hand. There is some utility, though: if economists are saying publicly that leading indicators for the economy are pointing in one direction or another then the direction for M&B will presumably be the same *if* the predictions of the economists are accurate.

"We wanted to find some leading indicators for M&B, meaning indicators you could look to that would give you an idea of where your market is headed and the course you'd likely be on if your operations continue steadily. That's what the succeeding two sets of correlations are designed to tell you.

"However, at first blush, it is surprising that the statistic for New Housing Permits within M&B's very own region of the country shows so little correlation over the same 11 years when it would seem to have a more direct relationship to M&B's revenues than GDP. Similarly, that last statistic—the Unemployment Rate—which is a generally accepted measure of economic health, also shows surprisingly little correlation over those 11 years.

"Those disparities surprised us, but when we took a second look at the two sets of statistics, paring our correlation down to the last five years *and* lagging the revenues against them by a year, the correlations mutated to being very strong. So, 96.78% as a coefficient of correlation for New Housing Permits intuitively makes a great deal of sense. Similarly, −99.61% is even stronger; remarkably so as that is almost a 1 to 1 inverse correlation; i.e. revenues and the National Unemployment Rate move in essentially opposite directions; that's why you have the minus sign for the coefficient. It's also logical. If unemployment is rising, that suggests there will be less income available for housing; and employers are not expanding or are even cutting jobs, signaling lower demand for their products and services, which in turn means less need for more commercial space. So we think we have identified two salient factors you should consider in your planning."

Mary spoke up. "Why should we think either one of those figures is reliable for 5 years when it's so unreliable for 11? Maybe those 5-year results are just a mathematical coincidence? I need a logical explanation if Bob and I are going to rely to any degree on monitoring those two statistics."

Joseph eagerly took up the challenge. "Mary, as usual, you are asking the right questions. The logical explanation is that in its earliest years, the effect of building revenue from a small base and a starting point of zero distorts the picture. Rather, once the Firm had established a comparable stability, the statistics fell into place. Secondarily, you rode out the turmoil of the Great Recession at a better rate than the one at which the GDP, New Housing Permits, and Unemployment statistics changed, which prevented the numbers—one might almost say coincidentally—from falling into place with a better correlation. It's also likely the case that M&B's revenue decline may have been fortuitously buffered to some extent by the government revenue in your mix during those years."

Bob rubbed his chin and said: "Yes, our government work has stayed pretty steady in dollars, but it's been a decreasing percentage as we've expanded the other two segments. That seems to jive, Joseph."

Alfred was anxious to drive the point home, as he opined: "What this means for M&B is that if you monitor the current *monthly* statistics released by the federal government for these two factors, New Housing Permits and Unemployment Rate, it seems very likely that you can anticipate whether your own revenues will be higher or lower one year from now and you can even set a target, which might be adjusted if you see a trend developing.

"Having two statistics is important because they should confirm one another. If they do not, it may mean that some kind of shift is taking place in economic relationships. Such a shift began in 2007 when the U.S. Federal Reserve System adopted so-called *Quantitative Easing*, which drove interest rates down via a major change in monetary policy and kept them at historically (some critics argue artificially) low levels. Consequently, the use of market interest rates as a leading indicator for many kinds of businesses became problematic.

"You might do some additional searching of your own for more than two—perhaps as many as half a dozen. We're trying to stay within budget so we stopped at two, but if more can be found that mathematically correlate, provided you can see a logical explanation that is not convoluted for why such correlation makes sense, the greater the confidence you can place on those signals.

"Of course, the goal is to do well in all economic periods—expansions and contractions, and booms and recessions. As a practice evolves and improves, it would hope to see more divergence from the downside of statistics and stronger relative performance against the statistics in better times. In that sense, what these statistics are indicating is the rise and fall of the market risk factor for you. When the risk is greater, you are more likely to be facing a difficult environment that would demand more marketing effort and greater cost control—two somewhat conflicting requirements. We'll address that conflict a little later today.

"Because those changes may occur or because economic relationships may shift, the statistics must not only be monitored but must also be considered from the vantage point of the Firm's relation to the market. Are there other signs emerging? For example, on the downside:

■ Are clients expressing concerns about being able to complete projects?

■ Have new inquiries for work slowed down?

- Are more calls seeking employment coming in?

- Have receivables payments slowed down?

- Are subs calling, looking for work?

- At professional meetings, are more people griping?

"On the upside, the questions and signs are just the reverse.

"Once or twice a year, we think you should use these statistics to help you set targets for revenue, which should naturally drive your overall budgeting and give you a touchstone for making decisions on major expenditures. However, if you see a new or counter trend developing that is confirmed by three months or more then those targets and budgets might be revisited and carefully adjusted.

"Of course, we'd expect you would not make adjustments on a 1 to 1 basis; indication of a 3% change in economic activity wouldn't mean you expect a 3% change in the same direction for revenue. No, what you'd want to do instead is look at the market opportunities you seem to have before you and decide if there are any signs they are at risk or if your fees might need to be adjusted. And, of course, whether that's a good time to be making planned expenditures, especially those aimed at expansion of capacity.

"Setting those targets and using them to budget and plan is where the second tool comes into play."

## LOOKING INWARD

The second tool, as described below by Sloan and Wharton, is one that's applicable to most any financial decision. Its power is in its simplicity because it can reduce any question to a calculation invoking the professional's common denominator: *time.*

No matter how much money is available, no matter how brilliant the professional, no matter the size of the firm or the popularity of the practice, every professional has but 168 hours per week in which to fit everything from sleep to work. Nor can time be doubled, accelerated, stretched, or otherwise manipulated. It is irrevocably fixed in quantity and accessibility at the rate of one, and only one, second per second. Hence, time is the scarcest and most precious resource of all.

So what is this tool and how does it work?

Perhaps it's easiest to demonstrate by example. One of the questions facing M&B is whether they should hire another administrative person, which would be an addition to overhead. The base costs for such a position would be:

| | |
|---|---|
| Salary | $30,000 |
| 14.6% Payroll Overhead | $4,380 |
| Base Cost | $34,380 |

On a monthly basis, that works out to $2,865/month. How will that be paid for? Earlier, we developed two important statistics:

Average Gross Profit Percentage = 45.22%[3]
Average Revenue Per Hour = $94.74/hour[4]

Putting the two together yields gross profit per average hour:

45.22% $\times$ $94.74 = $42.84/hour

So in each month, to cover the cost of an additional administrative person, it looks like this number of professional hours must be dedicated for that purpose:

$2,865/$42.84 = 66.88 hours

That seems like a significant commitment for such a small staff as it's more than a week of one professional's work (if the average workweek for M&B's professionals is 47.5 hours as was also determined earlier) and, in fact, more than two weeks' worth given the average billable time of 30.72 hours per week.[5]

However, there are some adjustments to be made. First, for this analysis, we want to look at gross profit exclusive of the 10% that is added on to subcontractor fees. Consequently, the adjustment revises the numbers from Exhibit 3.2 in a way that will be important in properly utilizing this tool:

**EXHIBIT 6.2** Net Professional Fee Gross Margin

|  | Residential | Commercial | Government | Total | % of Revenue |
|---|---|---|---|---|---|
| **Revenue ($)** | **638,324** | **719,381** | **188,436** | **1,546,141** |  |
| Subcontractor Expense ($) | 108,155 | 104,835 | 81,310 | 294,300 |  |
| Subcontractor Markup ($) | 10,816 | 10,484 | 8,131 | 29,430 |  |
| Net Professional Fee Revenue ($) | 519,354 | 604,063 | 98,995 | 1,222,411 | 100.00 |
| *Variable Costs* |  |  |  |  |  |
| Payroll ($) | 224,591 | 147,520 | 57,389 | 429,500 | 35.14 |
| Payroll Taxes ($) | 17,743 | 11,654 | 4,534 | 33,931 | 2.78 |
| Employee Benefits ($) | 27,903 | 18,328 | 7,130 | 53,361 | 4.37 |

3   Exhibit 3.2.
4   Exhibit 5.2.
5   Exhibit 5.7.

**EXHIBIT 6.2** *continued*

| | Residential | Commercial | Government | Total | % of Revenue |
|---|---|---|---|---|---|
| Print & Reproduction ($) | 3,093 | 4,210 | 5,691 | 12,994 | 1.06 |
| Unreimbursed Travel ($) | 4,045 | 10,496 | 8,326 | 22,867 | 1.87 |
| **Total Variable Costs ($)** | **277,375** | **192,208** | **83,070** | **552,652** | 45.21 |
| Variable Costs (%) | 53.41 | 31.82 | 83.91 | 45.21 | |
| | | | | | |
| **Gross Profit on Prof. Fees ($)** | **241,979** | **411,855** | **15,925** | **669,759** | 54.79 |
| *Gross Profit on Professional Fees (%)* | 46.59 | 68.18 | 16.09 | 54.79 | |

So in reality, each professional hour, averaging $94.74 in fees, is yielding a gross margin contribution equal to:

$94.74 × 54.79% = $51.91/hour

Consequently, the number of billable professional work hours needed to cover the base costs of this position still equals:

$2,865/$51.91 = 55.19 hours

But another adjustment is to take into account the extra professional time that will be required from Bob and/or Mary to hire and participate in some of the training for this person. That time is estimated to be a total of 20 hours between them in the first month and another 10 in the second.

On the other hand, once those two months are completed, the expectation is that the new administrator will conservatively save a total of 16 hours a month (roughly 4 per week) of Principal time. This saving is the conservative estimate to see if the position is justifiable.

The billing rate for both Bob and Mary is $150 per hour, so in terms of both the investment in the new position and the direct identifiable savings, the hourly gross profit calculation is:

$150 × 54.79% = $82.18/hour

How that looks over the course of the coming year is shown in Exhibit 6.3.

Basically, that's a continuing loss, which will continue indefinitely and get worse as the payroll costs for the new position go up, as they inevitably do over time.

However, Bob and Mary are not merely going to be performing more hourly work during that time. They assume instead that half that time will go to management duties and marketing efforts, which they estimate will yield one additional new project every other month.

Moreover, if M&B can raise fees per hour as planned on new projects, the gross profit percentage will move higher. The goal is an average rate of $110 per hour. Toward that end,

**EXHIBIT 6.3** Added Administrator Investment

| | | | | Per Hour Gross Profit | | | |
| Month | Base Cost | Hours<br>AddlSave | 82.18<br>Added Cost | Total Cost | 82.18<br>Saved | ProfitlLoss |
|---|---|---|---|---|---|---|
| 1 | 2,865 | 20 | 1,643 | 4,508 | 0 | –4,508 |
| 2 | 2,865 | 10 | 821 | 3,686 | 0 | –3,686 |
| 3 | 2,865 | –16 | 0 | 2,865 | 1,314 | –1,551 |
| 4 | 2,865 | –16 | 0 | 2,865 | 1,314 | –1,551 |
| 5 | 2,865 | –16 | 0 | 2,865 | 1,314 | –1,551 |
| 6 | 2,865 | –16 | 0 | 2,865 | 1,314 | –1,551 |
| 7 | 2,865 | –16 | 0 | 2,865 | 1,314 | –1,551 |
| 8 | 2,865 | –16 | 0 | 2,865 | 1,314 | –1,551 |
| 9 | 2,865 | –16 | 0 | 2,865 | 1,314 | –1,551 |
| 10 | 2,865 | –16 | 0 | 2,865 | 1,314 | –1,551 |
| 11 | 2,865 | –16 | 0 | 2,865 | 1,314 | –1,551 |
| 12 | 2,865 | –16 | 0 | 2,865 | 1,314 | –1,551 |
| Totals | 34,380 | –130 | 2,464 | 36,844 | 13,140 | –23,704 |

Bob and Mary each anticipate raising their own billing rate to $160 per hour, which, with 11 years in the marketplace, they believe they can realize.

They've also set the goal of raising the gross margin to 60% for their internal professional work; i.e. after adjusting for subcontractor fees that carry their anemic market-capped 10% markup. That's an increase in absolute terms of 60% – 54.79% = 5.21%. On a relative basis that works out at a 9.5%[6] improvement.

While 60% is a heroic target given the starting point, it's noteworthy that a rule of thumb for consultants to professional practices is that if rates charged for professionals are not equal to at least 2.5 times the *base salary*, the practice will be hard-pressed to make a profit; charging 2.5 times base salary means that gross profit on base salary should equal 60%.[7] In fact, M&B is merely trying to have all of its direct costs equal 60% of adjusted revenues. Is that realistic?

Right now, of each hour's revenue, direct costs consume:

$$DC = \$94.74 \times 45.21\% = \$42.83$$

If gross profit goes to 60% on average fee of $110/hour, gross profit becomes $66/hour. The remainder of the fee constitutes direct costs per hour, which would be $110 – $66 = $44.

---

6   5.21%/54.79% = 9.5%
7   2.5x = 100%; x = 40%

That's an increase in direct costs of only $1.17, which is a mere 2.73% increase from $42.83. That is clearly realistic, especially with a general inflation rate of 3% anticipated.

However, if staff is going to get raises, there's little room allowed for other direct costs to increase at all. On reflection, then, that does not seem like it's going to work.

Mary and Bob also recognize it will take some time to get the fee increases in place as existing projects are locked into lower rates, so the more realistic approach for this analysis is to assume that a material portion of the increase in gross margin can be achieved over the course of the year to work out to a gross profit of 57%, up almost 2.25% from 53.79%.

If the hourly fee for the principals is $160, the hourly gross margin at 57% equals a much healthier $91.20/hour for their billable time, while the average for all in the firm works out to:

$$\$110 \times 57\% = \$62.70$$

Recalling that each project has been yielding an average $6,435 per month in revenue,[8] that number would presumably increase by the 15.43% projected percentage increase in average fees.[9] With the additional information, newly supplied by Bob, that each project tends to last about 8 months, the coming year now looks quite different in a second cut:

**EXHIBIT 6.4** Added Administrator Investment: 2nd Cut

| 2nd CUT | | | Per Hour Gross Profit | | | | | |
|---|---|---|---|---|---|---|---|---|
| | | Hours | 91.20 | | 91.20 | | | |
| Month | Base Cost | Add\|Save | Added Cost | Total Cost | Saved | Marketing Benefit | Monthly Profit\|Loss | Cumulative Profit\|Loss |
| 1 | 2,865 | 20 | 1,824 | 4,689 | 0 | 0 | −4,689 | −4,689 |
| 2 | 2,865 | 10 | 912 | 3,777 | 0 | 0 | −3,777 | −8,466 |
| 3 | 2,865 | −16 | 0 | 2,865 | 1,459 | 0 | −1,406 | −9,872 |
| 4 | 2,865 | −16 | 0 | 2,865 | 1,459 | 4,234 | 2,828 | −7,044 |
| 5 | 2,865 | −16 | 0 | 2,865 | 1,459 | 4,234 | 2,828 | −4,216 |
| 6 | 2,865 | −16 | 0 | 2,865 | 1,459 | 8,468 | 7,062 | 2,846 |
| 7 | 2,865 | −16 | 0 | 2,865 | 1,459 | 8,468 | 7,062 | 9,908 |
| 8 | 2,865 | −16 | 0 | 2,865 | 1,459 | 12,702 | 11,296 | 21,204 |
| 9 | 2,865 | −16 | 0 | 2,865 | 1,459 | 12,702 | 11,296 | 32,500 |
| 10 | 2,865 | −16 | 0 | 2,865 | 1,459 | 16,936 | 15,530 | 48,030 |
| 11 | 2,865 | −16 | 0 | 2,865 | 1,459 | 16,936 | 15,530 | 63,560 |
| 12 | 2,865 | −16 | 0 | 2,865 | 1,459 | 21,170 | 19,764 | 83,324 |
| Totals | 34,380 | −130 | 2,736 | 37,116 | 14,592 | 105,848 | 83,324 | |

8  Exhibit 5.2.
9  Exhibit 5.6.

In other words, if M&B can make this scenario work, adding one project every other month and raising fees, then bringing in an additional Administrator will yield an additional $83,324 in *gross* profit, not net profit. (Overhead still has to be dealt with and will be later on in this chapter.) That makes the addition appear to be a very positive step.

The added administrator looks very appealing to everyone, but there's a fly in the ointment. The last column shows that it takes six months to recover the investment in the administrator and that the low point in this accounting comes in the third month when the net outflow accumulates to $9,872. The fly is bigger than that, though.

These numbers are book profit and loss numbers, *not* cash flow; and right now, cash flow is the biggest problem that M&B is facing. There is a plan to deal with that problem, primarily in the immediate future, by increasing collection efforts and driving down the age of receivables; but the plan has not yet been put into action, let alone succeeded. Bob and Mary have to consider the cash flow impact and that's the bigger fly, as the third cut at the calculations shows (Exhibit 6.5).

Looking again at the far right column, it's actually going to take 8 months to recover the investment in cash. Why? While the new projects may be signed up beginning in the fourth month, recall that an average collection time for receivables is 71 days,[10] so it will take about

**EXHIBIT 6.5** Added Administrator Investment: 3rd Cut

| 3rd CUT: CASH FLOW | | | Per Hour Gross Profit | | | | | |
|---|---|---|---|---|---|---|---|---|
| | | Hours | 91.20 | | | 91.20 | | |
| Month | Base Cost | Add\|Save | Added Cost | Total Cost | Saved | Marketing Benefit | Monthly Profit\|Loss | Cumulative Profit\|Loss |
| 1 | 2,865 | 20 | 1,824 | 4,689 | 0 | 0 | -4,689 | -4,689 |
| 2 | 2,865 | 10 | 912 | 3,777 | 0 | 0 | -3,777 | -8,466 |
| 3 | 2,865 | -16 | 0 | 2,865 | 1,459 | 0 | -1,406 | -9,872 |
| 4 | 2,865 | -16 | 0 | 2,865 | 1,459 | 0 | -1,406 | -11,278 |
| 5 | 2,865 | -16 | 0 | 2,865 | 1,459 | 0 | -1,406 | -12,683 |
| 6 | 2,865 | -16 | 0 | 2,865 | 1,459 | 4,234 | 2,828 | -9,855 |
| 7 | 2,865 | -16 | 0 | 2,865 | 1,459 | 4,234 | 2,828 | -7,027 |
| 8 | 2,865 | -16 | 0 | 2,865 | 1,459 | 8,468 | 7,062 | 35 |
| 9 | 2,865 | -16 | 0 | 2,865 | 1,459 | 8,468 | 7,062 | 7,097 |
| 10 | 2,865 | -16 | 0 | 2,865 | 1,459 | 12,702 | 11,296 | 18,393 |
| 11 | 2,865 | -16 | 0 | 2,865 | 1,459 | 12,702 | 11,296 | 29,689 |
| 12 | 2,865 | -16 | 0 | 2,865 | 1,459 | 16,936 | 15,530 | 45,219 |
| Totals | 34,380 | -130 | 2,736 | 37,116 | 14,592 | 67,743 | 45,219 | |

10  Exhibit 4.4.

2 months for that money to start coming in; thus the marketing benefit gets pushed back by two months. That makes the maximum cumulative cash flow hit in the fifth month with a nadir of $12,683.

This vignette illustrates why it's so important to consider the calculations in more than one accounting context. *Taking this question in isolation*, the administrator position should not be added until cash flow will permit it; but in isolation, it becomes a chicken and egg question because the better cash flow depends on biting the bullet and getting this position filled.

The question should not be taken in isolation but, rather, in the strategic context of the Firm's overall projections, including financing.

## PROFIT TARGET ANALYSIS

An additional administrator is an addition to overhead. Here is an example of that aforementioned conflict in requirements for more marketing effort and less costs writ large.

Where does overhead fit in the bigger picture of the Practice? What if the Practice improves its marketing or just lands a much bigger project that increases the administrative demands on Janet, who is the only administrator at present? What if she gets simply overwhelmed? Or becomes disabled? Or quits?

"In the past, I would have responded to questions like these intuitively," commented Mary. "Given that we're *not* making a ton of money yet we are working all the time, I'm open to a more rational approach."

Bob added: "I had no idea you could apply simple math and spreadsheets to such an extent to inform decision-making. It's elegant. Mary is right— since we started our practice, we've been over-relying on intuition to make everyday business decisions as well as those for longer-term planning. I always felt that intuition was undervalued, especially by all of you geeky MBA types, but this analytical process just makes so much sense. No offense, right Alfred? Some of our best friends are MBAs."

"No offense taken. Some of *our* best friends are artsy, prima donna, academic types who only wear black," said Wharton, tongue in cheek.

Quickly redirecting the conversation, Sloan said: "You ain't seen nothin' yet. Wait until you understand our Profit Target Analysis."

Sloan and Wharton then launched into their explanation of another useful tool. This hourly tool has a second function, playing a role in what is classically called *Breakeven Analysis* but which might well be referred to as *Profit Target Analysis*. In that process, overhead is now, at last, also considered. Here's how it works, looking backward at M&B's recent year end as reformatted in Exhibit 3.2 and Exhibit 6.2 as well as at some of the other exhibits that have been developed in the preceding chapters:

**EXHIBIT 6.6** Breakeven Analysis

| |
|---|
| **Breakeven Revenues = R** |
| **Breakeven Professional Hours = H** |
| **Subcontractor Revenues = S = $294,300** |
| **Subcontractor Contribution = 10% $\times$ S = SC = $29,430** |
| **Gross Profit Margin = GM = 54.79%** |
| **Total Overhead = F = $712,808** |
| **Adjusted Fixed Costs\* = AF** |
| **Average Professional Standard Hour Fee = P = $94.74** |
| **Average Professional Hour Direct Cost = $42.95** |
| **Average Professional Hour Gross Profit = $51.91** |

| STEP #1: | Adjust Fixed Costs for Subcontractor Gross Profit |
|---|---|
| | F – SC = $712,808 – $29,430 = AF = **$683,378** |

| STEP #2: | Calculate Gross Breakeven Revenues |
|---|---|
| | Breakeven Revenues = Adjusted Fixed Costs/Gross Margin |
| | R = AF/GM |
| | R = $683,378/54.79% = |
| | **Breakeven Revenues = $1,247,268** |

| STEP #3: | Calculate Billable Hours Needed per Year to Break Even |
|---|---|
| | Billable Hours = Revenues/Average Professional Hourly Fee |
| | H = R/P |
| | H = $1,247,268/$94.74 = |
| | **Needed Billable Hours = 13,165** |

| STEP #4: | PROOFS | |
|---|---|---|
| *DOLLARS:* | Breakeven Revenues = 13,165 $\times$ $94.74 = | $1,247,252 |
| | Less: Direct Costs = 13,165 $\times$ $42.83 = | $563,857 |
| | Gross Profit | $683,395 |
| | Less: Adjusted Overhead | $683,378 |
| | **BREAKEVEN Net** (Rounding Difference) | **$17** |

**EXHIBIT 6.6** *continued*

| HOURS: | Breakeven Hours | 13,165 |
|---|---|---|
| | Less: Actual Hours Billed | −12,906 |
| | Hours Short | 259 |
| | Multiply by Gross Profit/Hour | $51.91 |
| | **Calculated Loss** | **$13,453** |
| Rounding Difference | **Actual Loss** | **$13,620**** |

Notes: * For simplicity's sake, the assumption is made here that fixed costs are equal to overhead. That is true for the most part—but not always. A firm's accounting ought to be scrutinized to be sure that costs are accurately differentiated and identified as to being fixed or variable.

** The rounding difference of $167 is somewhat large, but this arises through the cumulative effects of using whole hours and two place decimals for dollars and percentage rates in the earlier calculations and tables from which the key statistics are derived. For firms with larger magnitudes of dollar figures, fractional cents and more refined percentages can yield more material differences.

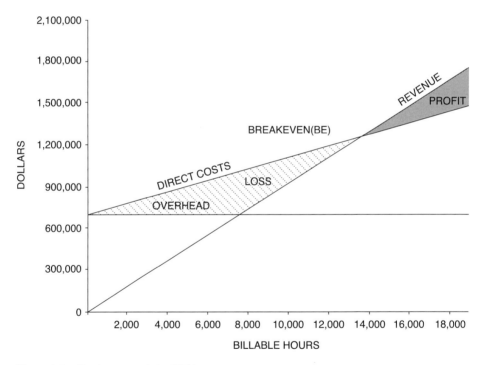

**Figure 6.1**   Breakeven graph for 20XX.

This information can be displayed graphically, the Breakeven Point arising where the Revenue line intersects the sum of the Fixed Overhead line and the correspondingly climbing Direct Cost line. That point is identified as "BE" on Figure 6.1. To the left of the BE point, the Firm is losing money if Billable Hours are fewer; and to the right, the Firm is making a profit.

Those potential profit and loss numbers are represented by the vertical distance between the Revenue line and the sum of the two cost lines.

That backward-looking information is interesting, but that's not where the power of this tool lies. After all, we already know that the Firm lost $13,620 last year. It does tell us a little, though. We can figure out that at the rates charged, if the Firm had billed 259 more hours then it would have broken even. That's only 2% (259/12,906) more!

The other way to look at this is to ask, "What fee rate would have yielded breakeven with the number of hours that were billed?" That would be $1,247,252/12,906 hours = $96.64. Of course, since that's the other half of the revenue equation (Rate $\times$ Hours = Revenues) it means the same 2% increase.[11]

If both increased by 1% then breakeven would also have been met:

$$(101\% \times 12,906 \text{ hours}) \times (101\% \times \$94.74) =$$
$$13,035 \text{ hours} \times \$95.69 = \$1,247,319$$

Now we want to repeat that process but with new information developed throughout the consultation with Sloan and Wharton.

One key question is the input for overhead. Two major elements of that expense group are whether and when the two new positions of Marketing Specialist and Assistant Administrator will be added.

Another key question is capacity. Adding projects is great, but someone has to do the work. As people are added, some of the overhead costs (which are assumed to be fixed) will become unfixed; i.e. more money has to be spent to support the additional professional staff as well as the existing staff.

One of those critical overhead expenses that will vary once three or more people are added is rent since there simply isn't enough space under the current lease. For a little while, that shortfall can be juggled by having staff share desks and work remotely, but it's clear that efficiency will suffer to some degree and the risk of error increases. For M&B, it turns out that there is space available within their present building; if the firm takes that added space for the whole year then the rent costs will increase by 20%.

So with the help of Sloan and Wharton, the Firm comes up with the following tentative decisions, which need to be tested:

- The Marketing Specialist is assumed to cost $48,000 for a year and will be brought on at the start of the fourth month, for a salary cost of $36,000 for the year.

- The second Administrator will be hired to start as soon as possible, with a salary of $34,000.

---

11   $96.64 – $94.74 = $1.90; $1.90/$94.74 = 2%

- Another Intern will be brought on at the start of the second quarter to increase capacity, also assuming that projects have increased as expected.

- The extra people will also add $750 in software licensing fees, part of the Computer Expenses line item.

- Accordingly, with the same revenue assumptions, the additional space will be acquired at the start of the second quarter as well, yielding a 15% addition to rent (three-quarters of the 20% for the whole year) on top of the regularly scheduled 3% increase (i.e. an overall increase of $1.03 \times 1.15 = 1.1815\%$).

- The added space will require $33,000 in additional expenditures for furniture and equipment, but to conserve cash, after an initial deposit of $3,000, all will be leased for $933 per month, or an additional $8,400 for the year.

- The added space will also generate a 12% annual increase (so for 9 months, which is three-quarters of the year, this is 9%) in utilities on top of the 3% budgeted increase (i.e. $1.03 \times 1.09 = 1.1227\%$).

- The added individuals and added space will further yield proportional increases to employee benefits and insurance costs.

- All other overhead expenses are budgeted for a 3% increase.

- As already indicated, the assumption is that project fees can be raised to an average of $110/hour, *but* phasing in those increases with the current mix of projects is calculated to work out over the course of the year to an average of only $104/hour.

- Similarly, and as discussed above, direct cost controls yield an average projected gross margin of 57% for the year; a decided improvement but not the 60% desired.

- Lastly, the expectation is that subcontractor revenue will rise to only $300,000 as more effort is made to limit subcontractor expense.

Given those assumptions, Exhibit 6.7 shows how the overhead will look.

With that calculation made, what does a new Breakeven Analysis suggest for the coming year? (See Exhibit 6.8.)

Once again, these results can be graphed in the same manner, displaying a new Breakeven Point (see Figure 6.2).

With the fee increases in place and the better control over direct costs to further improve gross margin, the exciting result is that the number of additional billable hours needed to get to breakeven seems achievable. Last year, 12,906[12] hours were billed, so an increase of only 713 hours is needed to get to 13,619 breakeven hours. Of that, roughly 130 are projected

---

12   See Exhibit 5.7.

**EXHIBIT 6.7** Overhead Projection for Next Year

| | 20XX | Added Cost | Next Year Cost |
|---|---|---|---|
| Advertising & Promotion | 12,029 | 361 | 12,390 |
| Automobile Expense | 9,859 | 296 | 10,155 |
| Bad Debts | 34,100 | 1,023 | 35,123 |
| Bank Charges | 2,895 | 87 | 2,982 |
| Charitable Contributions | 2,000 | 60 | 2,060 |
| Computer Expenses | 17,702 | 1,281 | 18,983 |
| Consultants | 24,000 | 720 | 24,720 |
| Depreciation & Amortization | 62,089 | 1,863 | 63,952 |
| Dues | 16,200 | 486 | 16,686 |
| Employee Benefits | 12,113 | 12,120 | 24,233 |
| Equipment Lease | 8,836 | 8,400 | 17,236 |
| Insurance | 42,108 | 2,526 | 44,634 |
| Interest | 16,545 | 496 | 17,041 |
| Legal & Accounting | 23,942 | 718 | 24,660 |
| Licenses | 5,250 | 0 | 5,250 |
| Maintenance | 12,880 | 386 | 13,266 |
| Meals & Entertainment | 47,154 | 1,415 | 48,569 |
| Miscellaneous Expense | 19,245 | 577 | 19,822 |
| Office Expense | 16,893 | 507 | 17,400 |
| Outside Services | 8,750 | 263 | 9,013 |
| Payroll—Nonprofessional | 97,500 | 70,000 | 167,500 |
| Payroll Taxes | 7,681 | 5,643 | 13,324 |
| Penalties | 1,807 | 54 | 1,861 |
| Rent | 50,880 | 9,387 | 60,267 |
| Repairs & Warranties | 11,014 | 330 | 11,344 |
| Subscriptions | 18,540 | 556 | 19,096 |
| Supplies | 23,303 | 699 | 24,002 |
| Taxes | 19,909 | 597 | 20,506 |
| Telephone & Fax | 27,516 | 825 | 28,341 |
| Training & Seminars | 16,860 | 506 | 17,366 |
| Overhead Travel | 32,000 | 960 | 32,960 |
| Utilities | 11,208 | 1,375 | 12,583 |
| | | | |
| Total Overhead | 712,808 | 124,519 | 837,327 |

**EXHIBIT 6.8** Breakeven Projection for Next Year

**Breakeven Revenues = R**

**Breakeven Professional Hours = H**

**Gross Profit Margin = GM = 57.00%**

**Fixed Costs = Overhead = F = $837,327**

**Average Professional Std, Hourly Fee = P = $104.00**

**Average Professional Hour Direct Cost = C = $44.72**

**Average Professional Hour Gross Profit = $59.28**

**Subcontractor Revenue = S = $300,000**

**Subcontractor Gross Profit = SC = $30,000**

| STEP #1: | Calculate Adjusted Overhead to Cover |
| | Adjusted Fixed Costs = F − SC |
| | $837,327 − $30,000 = $807,327 |

| STEP #2: | Calculate Gross Breakeven Revenues |
| | Breakeven Revenues = Fixed Costs/Gross Margin |
| | R = F/GM |
| | R = $807,327/57% |
| | R = $1,416,363 |

| STEP #3: | Calculate Billable Hours per Year to Break Even |
| | H = R/P |
| | H = $1,416,363/$104 |
| | H = 13,618.88 Billable Hours |

| STEP #4: | PROOF | |
| | Fee Revenues = 13,618.88 × $104 = | $1,416,363 |
| | Subcontractor Markup | $30,000 |
| | Total Revenues | $1,446,363 |
| | Less: Direct Costs = 13,618.88 × $43.86 = | −$609,036 |
| | Gross Profit | $837,327 |
| | Less: Overhead | −$837,327 |
| | Profit = BREAKEVEN | **$0** |

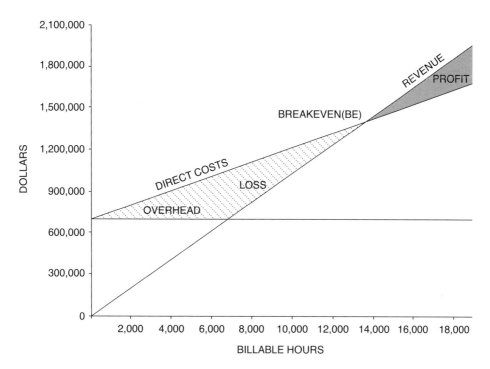

**Figure 6.2** Breakeven graph for next year.

to be picked up by the Principals (per Exhibit 6.5), meaning that only 583 additional billable hours are needed from staff, including the new Intern. Given that the new Intern should also average 47.5 hours of work time per week for 9 months, there are 1,852.5 hours available in the forecast; so if the Intern alone has to pick up all the slack, that new employee needs to be 583/1852.5 = 31.5% efficient in yielding billable hours. That gives a pretty fair amount of time for training to get the Intern up to speed and still do better.[13]

Now this is the point where the analysis becomes especially trenchant because the goal is *not* breakeven; it is to generate *profit!* How much? Bob and Mary just need to decide what they want in profits and it's easy to make a calculation based on what we already know. The basic formula is:

(Adjusted Fixed Costs + Profit)/Gross Margin = Revenue Target

However (does it seem like when we're ready for profits, there's always a *however?*), the practical limits created by constraints on capacity—staffing, space, equipment, etc.—must

---

13 If there's fixed fee work involved, all that's necessary is to convert fixed fees to a net hourly rate by first subtracting all budgeted direct costs from the fixed fees and then dividing by budgeted hours to determine the hourly rate. Of course, if the budgeted hours are off-target, the actual results will vary: worse if work takes longer; better if accomplished under budget.

**EXHIBIT 6.9** Potential Profit Targets for Next Year

| | Breakeven | Target A | Target B | Target C |
|---|---|---|---|---|
| Gross Profit Margin (%) | 57.00 | 57.00 | 57.00 | 57.00 |
| Overhead Projected ($) | 837,327 | 837,327 | 837,327 | 837,327 |
| Less: Subcontractor Markup ($) | −30,000 | −30,000 | −30,000 | −30,000 |
| Target Profit ($) | 0 | 100,000 | 200,000 | 300,000 |
| Subtotal: Overhead to be Covered ($) | 807,327 | 907,327 | 1,007,327 | 1,107,327 |
| Covering Revenue at 57% GM ($) | 1,416,363 | 1,591,802 | 1,767,240 | 1,942,679 |
| | | | | |
| Hourly Average Rate ($) | 104.00 | 104.00 | 104.00 | 104.00 |
| Hours Needed | 13,619 | 15,306 | 16,993 | 18,680 |
| | | | | |
| # Professionals | 9.25 | 9.25 | 9.25 | 9.25 |
| Hours/Year/Professional Needed | 1,472.31 | 1,654.68 | 1,837.05 | 2,019.42 |
| Hours/Week/Professional Needed | 28.31 | 31.82 | 35.33 | 38.83 |
| At 75% Efficiency on 47.5 Hours | 35.62 | 35.62 | 35.62 | 35.62 |
| Hours Cushion | 7.31 | 3.80 | 0.30 | −3.21 |
| | | | | |
| Realistic? | **YES** | **YES** | **YES** | **NO** |

**EXHIBIT 6.10** Profit Potential at Peak Efficiencies

| | Peak Efficiency (%) | | | |
|---|---|---|---|---|
| | **70.0** | **72.5** | **75.0** | **80.0** |
| # Professionals | 9.25 | 9.25 | 9.25 | 9.25 |
| Billable Hrs. per 47.5 Hrs. Workweek | 33.2500 | 34.4325 | 35.6250 | 38.0000 |
| Maximum Hours at Peak Efficiency | 307.56 | 318.55 | 329.53 | 351.50 |
| Times Average Hourly Fee ($) | 104 | 104 | 104 | 104 |
| Maximum Weekly Revenue ($) | 31,987 | 33,129 | 34,271 | 36,556 |
| Maximum Yearly Revenue ($) | 1,663,298 | 1,722,702 | 1,782,105 | 1,900,912 |
| Times Gross Profit Margin (%) | 57.00 | 57.00 | 57.00 | 57.00 |
| Gross Profit on Professional Fees ($) | 948,080 | 981,940 | 1,015,800 | 1,083,520 |
| Subcontractor Markup ($) | $30,000 | $30,000 | $30,000 | $30,000 |
| Total Gross Profit ($) | 978,080 | 1,011,940 | 1,045,800 | 1,113,520 |
| Overhead Projected ($) | −837,327 | −837,327 | −837,327 | −837,327 |
| Profit at Peak Efficiency ($) | 140,753 | 174,613 | 208,473 | 276,193 |

be considered. The overhead costs that are fixed for a while, like our administrative staff and facilities cost, are semi-variable over time with changes in size and other dynamics. With that reality momentarily in the background, Exhibit 6.9 shows some potential profit targets based on the current profile of the Firm.

Target C of a $300,000 profit is not realistic because there is not enough capacity to bring in that much revenue. The flip side of the question is to simply derive the maximum profit at full practical efficiency or, better yet, to consider the possible range of practical average peak efficiencies over the course of the year (Exhibit 6.10).

By now, the power of breakeven should be apparent as the fundamental metrics identified by the interplay of revenue components and elements (i.e. hours, fee rate, markup), direct costs, gross profit margin and overhead can be manipulated and modeled using an ordinary spreadsheet program for planning, operating, monitoring, and control; in short, as a critical management tool.

Naturally, the figures foretold are one part of the battle, but the greater follow-on challenge is to determine and execute the *how* of making the performance match the forecast figures. Winning the projects, satisfying the client while delivering at no more than budgeted direct costs, collecting the revenues (no small challenge sometimes) and keeping the hungry overhead pit bull from devouring the hard-earned gross profit must be managed with all the concomitant pieces of marketing, operations, and administration duly coordinated and supporting one another.

One ancillary twist based on gross margin is its utility for promoting overhead control. Every expenditure that will not be recovered as a direct cost (which also must be controlled to maintain gross margin) must be paid for out of the gross profit produced by hourly revenues. For example, assume for M&B's consideration, an expenditure of $570 to add another shared printer to the computer network since staff occasionally get backed up on printer jobs:

Billable Hours = (Expense/Gross Margin)/Average Hourly Fee
Billable Hours = ($570/57%)/$104
Billable Hours = 9.62 hours

Hence, the question becomes, "Is this expense worth exclusively devoting 9.62 billable hours of time and revenue?" Experience shows this is a particularly useful exercise for responding to staff requests for expenditures. When staff understands the impact of expenditures, this is a material help in engaging their cooperation. Moreover, when there is the kind of compensation system that is tied to Firm and individual profit performance, the likelihood becomes much greater that staff will cooperatively—even enthusiastically—participate in controlling costs at all levels.

# WHAT ABOUT RISK MANAGEMENT?

Sloan introduced the topic of risk management by first stating the obvious. "Even though this is self-evident, it is so important it's worth declaring emphatically: Having great relationships with clients, contractors, sub-consultants, and others who work on a project will significantly enrich projects *and* facilitate addressing problems expeditiously. Being on good terms with all these people will help to avoid claims and resolve conflicts. Moreover, it will help prevent any conflicts that do arise from escalating to the point where lawyers and insurance

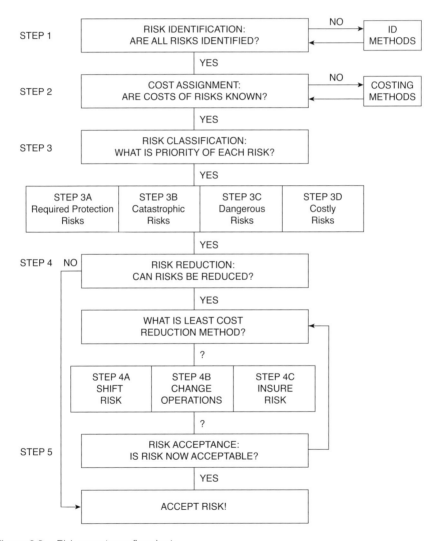

**Figure 6.3** Risk acceptance flowchart.

companies are compelled to get involved. So, the take-home message is to establish and maintain rapport and to respect everyone on the design and construction teams."

"In other words," Wharton added, "self-absorbed prima donnas will, for the most part, be unsuccessful in business matters."

Mary shifted restlessly in her seat. "He can't possibly be talking about us, right, Bob?"

"Yep." Bob then turned toward Joseph while brushing the crumbs of what remained of his scone from his black turtleneck. "So, other than being the charismatic, charming, and genuinely nice people that we are, what else should we be thinking about to protect ourselves from risk?"

Sloan and Wharton then presented a fairly concise tutorial on risk management as follows.

Modeling offers some opportunity to consider the effect of risk in planning and forecasting, but that modeling merely identifies what the impact of various risks may be if they come to pass. That's just the first step in risk management, albeit an important one. It does not provide guidance for finding a way to delimit the risk or to mitigate the impact of negative consequences arising from disadvantageous events. The steps in managing risk are portrayed in Figure 6.3.

As Figure 6.3 illustrates, risks are identified in Step 1, cost for each is assigned in Step 2, and if the risks become reality then they are classified in Step 3 in one of four ways:

1. **Required Protection Risks** are those that must be insured (e.g. worker compensation insurance if employees are employed) or eliminated (e.g. practicing engineering without an engineering license).

2. **Catastrophic Risks** are those that will effectively destroy the firm (e.g. a massive malpractice lawsuit that is lost).

3. **Dangerous Risks**, while not terminating the enterprise, will severely handicap it, effectively reducing its potential (e.g. a publicized malpractice lawsuit that is lost, damaging reputation and costing substantial amounts in expenses, time, and damages).

4. **Costly Risks**, while unfortunate and engendering of expense, are in the nature of an ongoing business expense (e.g. an employee's fender bender auto accident while on Firm business for which the Firm is liable).

These classifications set the priorities for addressing the risks. Step 4 recognizes there are three and only three fundamental ways to manage risk:

1. insure risk;

2. shift risk contractually;[14]

3. change operations to minimize or mitigate risk.

---

14  Some may well argue that insurance is just a form of contractually shifting risk as the insurance policy is a specialized form of contract. Nevertheless, because it is specialized for risk management, it is identified separately.

Otherwise, when all is said and done, the default choice is Step 5—accept risk.

Insurance, of course, has a direct premium cost that can be adjusted for policy limits, deductibles, co-insurance, exclusions, and other policy features that yield coverage. The amounts for which the insured is liable (e.g. deductibles, losses in excess of limits, etc.) remain as exposures to risk. Adjustments in policy terms should be aimed at creating a balanced mix of coverage and premiums to affordably fend off at least the Catastrophic Risks and hopefully Dangerous Risks as well. A good insurance agent and/or insurance consultant (the latter of which introduces an additional cost akin to premiums) should be able to offer expert assistance. It is important to actually read insurance policies to be sure their coverage, exclusions, deductibles, and conditions are clearly understood and properly addressed in the course of developing operational strategies and tactics.

The second alternative of shifting risk has the potential primary cost of being unable to reach agreement for a contract with the other party. A secondary cost for legal help to make the risk-shifting work as intended can also add to the consideration of cost. If that other party is a prospective client who will not abide by the proffered contract, the opportunity cost may be substantial. Conversely, if the Firm retains or shares in risks with regard to other parties to a project, including the Firm's own subcontractors, costs can also be engendered if those risks come to pass.

Balancing the opportunities against the risks is management's job. It should be evident that if insurance coverage is inadequate and if the immediate pressures for revenue unduly skew managerial judgment toward accepting more risk, then risk-taking becomes more perilous.

The third alternative of changing operations also can be costed and compared against existing expenses. For example, if the issue is delimiting malpractice, perhaps there are procedures for additional reviews that might be adopted or computer programs that might be employed to verify mathematical calculations. If so, the costs introduced by each must be considered.

The many statistical, stochastic, and algorithmic methods for selecting the best mix of insurance, contractual terms, operational adjustments, and risk acceptance are, regrettably, beyond the scope of this book. Suffice it to say, however, that attention to this detail is a responsibility for the Principals.

## FINANCING

All of the activities and all of the plans require capital to implement. The plans for additional personnel and their concomitant support additions all mean money must be on hand for funding.

Back in Chapter 4, introduction was made of a *rolling cash flow budget* (Exhibit 4.6), which was adjusted for improved collections of accounts receivable in arrears (Exhibit 4.7). As the

Breakeven and Profit Target model is massaged and refined once a strategy is identified for adoption, the data it produces can be included in the rolling cash flow budget to see whether or not it appears the Firm will have the necessary funds on hand when the necessary expenses are due to be paid. If this critical planning step is missed or mismanaged, a Firm can literally grow itself into bankruptcy.

If there's a shortfall, a mechanism for funding has to be found or the strategy has to be changed. The alternatives for funding often come down to just these:

1. **Borrowing from a bank or other financial institution.** This alternative, particularly when dealing with the acquisition of equipment, vehicles, or other assets, includes leasing from or through the vendor.

2. **Stretching out payables.** This tactic is the same as utilizing trade credit, but over-stretching will ultimately harm the Firm's credit reputation and make future funding that much more problematic.

3. **Collecting receivables more quickly.** It may be possible to develop and obtain agreement for more accelerated payment schedules as well as to negotiate for payment incentives and advance deposits as discussed in Chapter 4. Frequently, the primary focus should be on the clients that have adopted the tactic of stretching out payments owed to the Practice. Client relations and market reputation demand a degree of delicacy and wise but practical sensitivity in dealing with collections. Because of the nature of projects and the relationship of owners to their financing lenders, there may be practical limits to what can be accomplished without burning bridges, which can create additional risks and attendant costs.

4. **Self-funding through Principals putting money into the Firm's coffers.** Whether accounted for as loans, deferred pay, equity, or otherwise, self-funding has unique and material tax attributes that arise both when money is paid in and when it is paid back, which—wittingly or unwittingly—can make this an attractive or a deeply unpleasant alternative. Assessing the tax characteristics and implications is critical before pulling the trigger on putting money in. Additionally, where there are multiple owners, the relationship among them can easily be strained when there are differences in financial ability and attitude.

With the possible exception of the fourth option, once the commitment is made, the future cash flow projections (i.e. the budget) has to pick up the expenditures of cash to repay the funding. The structure of repayments and the appreciation of operational risks that might upset the plans may make the self-funding option, in particular, a less than optimal choice because some last resort cash resource should be kept in reserve to deal with calamities and, some would say, unanticipated great opportunities.

The good news is that if the growth is achieved on target, the additional cash should be available to make repayment or the return on the self-funding investment without undue strain.

Whether such growth will be wise or not is one more risk to consider, and in that sense, the reliability of leading indicators (e.g. M&B's Exhibit 6.1) can be a key factor in evaluating that risk.

## OTHER CONSTRAINTS

Other than an occasional nod, little has been discussed regarding taxes—especially, but not only, income taxes. Nor have the exhibits reflected any more than the most cursory information on tax requirements. This minimal treatment is not an oversight.

The frequent changes imposed by legislation, regulation, and judicial interpretation place any discussion in this format at serious risk of prompt, even misleading, obsolescence. Additionally, the many state, local, and foreign jurisdictions that may want a tax bite prohibit any but the most limited generalization. That limited generalization is to stress the need for competent tax advice.

In a similar vein, changing non-tax regulatory, licensing, and ethical standards for professionals and their practices present another constraint on what may be realistically achievable on the profits and financial front. Those with residential practices may face particular demands on what's practical in operation because of frequently changing and sometimes conflicting zoning, land use, environmental, and consumer protection efforts. The bottom line on these regulatory and ethical standards is that they often affect the practice's bottom line by imposing additional costs that, by law or market force, might not be passed on to the client or, otherwise, not be avoidable or fully recoverable. As a footnote to the earlier brief discussion about risk, these kinds of concerns have great attraction for risk-shifting to subcontractors and other contractual participants.

Lastly and counterintuitively, growth can impose its own sort of backlash constraint. While growth is usually desirable, if not essential, to a practice's health, it nevertheless creates temporary distortions, intermittent diseconomies, and disruption in routines. Like a car that accelerates too quickly for the driver to maintain control, faster growth tends to generate unforeseen challenges.

Moreover, as new financial territory is explored in the northeast corner of a graph of profits, formerly stable relationships among metrics can mutate into the unexpected. Not all relationships are linearly or even stably scalable. Some may not be scalable at all. Semi-variable costs, with their sudden jump in expenditures mandating other expenditures, represent one example of that nonlinear phenomenon. The additions to staff of the Marketing Specialist and second Administrator generate the need for more space, which has to be filled with furniture and office equipment. In turn, covering the cost of that new overhead demands at least one addition to professional staff to yield adequate capacity, all with the implicit assumption that remunerative project contracts can be generated at an adequate rate to profitably use, but not overload, that capacity.

The successful managers of the business side of the practice will be those whose intuition, spurred on by frequent monitoring of accurately reported data, provides early alerts. Those alerts command that precious resource of *time* in order to address those changes, distortions, diseconomies, and disruptions with appropriate decisional and operational adjustments.

Such adjustments are not always mathematically derivable or statistically certain. Subjectivity, an inevitable factor in all professional endeavors—as in life—is considered in the next chapter, together with some ideas about transforming practices in an innovative and entrepreneurial fashion.

**7**

# RETHINKING PRACTICE: TACTICAL INNOVATIONS FOR FINANCIAL PROSPERITY AND PROFESSIONAL SATISFACTION

*Creativity is the root of entrepreneurship.*
—**Karndee Leopairote**[1]

*What we need to do is learn to work in the system, by which I mean that everybody, every team, every platform, every division, every component is there not for individual competitive profit or recognition, but for contribution to the system as a whole on a win-win basis.*
—**W. Edwards Deming**[2]

The previous chapters have discussed key financial and business strategies to ensure health and prosperity for the Practice. Now that this essential foundation for success has been set forth, we

1   Cited in Madanmohan Rao, "Creativity and Entrepreneurship: 30 Inspiring Quotes on Innovation," October 17, 2014, http://yourstory.com/2014/10/creativity-30-quotes/

2   www.quotationspage.com/quote/26355.html

are free to examine possibilities for designing innovative, *entrepreneurial* practice models with concomitantly appropriate profit margins that will provide increased professional satisfaction as well as profitability.

We want to state the premise of this chapter as clearly and emphatically as possible: that designing (or redesigning) and operating a business should be as creative and compelling as designing and constructing a building. Indeed, there are many innovative, entrepreneurial opportunities that can be discovered and developed to enrich a practice.

## THE BIG PICTURE: WHAT'S PROFITABLE, WHAT'S ENJOYABLE—CAN THEY INTERSECT?

Let's revisit Bob and Mary's aspirations for M&B Architects listed at the beginning of Chapter 2. Underlying M&B's financial challenges is a certain restlessness and frustration with the work itself. Sloan and Wharton recommended that Bob and Mary dust off their mission and vision statements and re-evaluate what they want to do in terms of both the nature of the work and income. Sloan underscored the importance of integrating and leveraging the passions of current staff into the Practice as part of this exercise. Wharton implored them to consider conducting this inaugural review as a next step, one that ideally will be updated annually.

Bob jumped in: "I think we have a pretty good list of statements about our general philosophical approach to doing architecture, which, by the way, does not really distinguish us from every other design-oriented architecture firm on the planet. But I get the feeling that's not enough in today's world. For one thing, I'm not all that happy with the projects I'm overseeing, which are, frankly, mundane back porch–like additions or small office suites for clients who are not in search of design that moves the spirit. Providing comprehensive services for small-scale projects like these are not very profitable, and the design time—the fun part for me—is miniscule. Not only that, I'm spending too much time on administrative issues for the Firm (which, thankfully, we now have a chance of correcting). Mary, I know you're also not exactly dancing around the office these days."

Mary launched her own diatribe. "Indeed, Bob. I'm frustrated because I want the blue-chip clients who dangle larger-scale projects, and who *are* interested in high-quality design. But they are so elusive; I'm not sure why they don't want to even consider hiring us. Maybe we're too focused on traditional architectural design. That's what we were trained to do, but the power of design thinking and a design education enables us to solve myriad other client problems. How do we plug in to what clients really want? So, Alfred and Joseph—as our business gurus who are getting the big bucks—can you give us some direction about becoming more entrepreneurial to procure the commissions we want and that have better margins? Can you help us to apply our natural creativity and design thinking to new business models and opportunities?"

# ENTREPRENEURIAL PRACTICE MODELS

"This is exactly where the rubber meets the road," said Joseph Sloan bluntly. "You've completed enough self-analysis and reflection to *finally* ask the right questions and have an attitude that leads you to *embrace* change in order to prosper in today's challenging business environment. Alfred and I were hoping you would arrive at this point (with a little subtle direction from us) so that you would be excited and invested in pursuing new heights in practice with your feet on the ground. By 'feet on the ground' I mean that you are well prepared—and this is, and always has been, our mantra—to make wise business decisions informed by financial basics and tools (as described in previous chapters). Going forward, I implore you—as only you two can do as creative architects—to view the development of new practice models as a unique design problem for *your* Firm."

Sloan continued his discourse. "You recall that the Profit Target Analysis works fine *if* your marketing efforts are successful. Hiring a Marketing Specialist aids those efforts; but, when all is said and done, the Marketing Specialist can only succeed if the steak is there with the sizzle. In other words, what the Firm delivers must be seen by the client as—and in fact be—worth the fee. That's ultimately the foundation for good client relations, good reputations, growth, and lasting profitability. So we have ideas about some ways to envision, select, package, promote, and perform M&B's services.

"Some of the ideas we're going to discuss come from the profession's literature, others are from other professions, and some are our own. To a very great extent in considering these suggestions, we've looked for ideas that require little to no additional expenditure but, rather, can be adopted by reframing and/or redeploying the resources you already have. We recommend that you use the analytical financial tools that we've outlined to model and test the ideas you find appealing and to set realistic targets and budgets for monitoring of implementation and ongoing utilization."

Sloan said that he and Wharton believe these ideas offer innovative practice models and can also trigger creative thinking. Distinctiveness and competitive advantage will be a function of the specific expertise, skill sets, and personalities of the Firm. Building on some of these ideas and inventing new ones are intended to disrupt the Practice status quo in order to spring into an exhilarating and lucrative future:

1. ***Establish a super-consultancy and offer a spectrum of services on a project basis.*** One way to get more and better clients is to provide additional services so the client truly believes that they only need to hire one firm, with the highest degree of excellence, to solve *all* their problems. You can engage in the exhilarating architectural design that you love to do as one of those services, but also coordinate expert consultants to address clients' other needs and requirements. In this super-consultancy model, you build on your core services by applying design thinking, along with a host of highly skilled specialists, to solve myriad client-related problems.

A super-consultancy is created by setting up alliances—both virtual and physical—with experts who complement existing skills and who can focus on the specific issues either articulated by the prospective client or surmised by the alliance.[3] The super-consultancy can open up new markets including previously unexplored building types, larger-scale jobs, projects with highly technical demands, and work for clients in search of a range of pre-design and/or post-construction services.

Collectively, the talents comprising a strategic alliance can be very powerful. The combination of seasoned professionals with those who provide fresh perspectives could make a convincing argument for providing the best services—and value—for many clients. Here are a few examples (in no particular order) of specialized services that might spark ideas for the Practice.

- Engage in building commissioning to ensure all systems are working to maximize user comfort together with optimal energy savings.

- Conduct pre- and post-occupancy evaluations to quantify benefits of newly designed space.

- Team with commercial real estate brokers for tenant improvements.

- Collaborate with a good constructor for clients who seek design–build project delivery.

- Associate with developers (see "Smart Fees", below); engage in speculative real estate development.

- Offer a range of facilities planning services, such as maintenance plans and scheduling, and energy optimization strategies.

- Identify and then assist clients to navigate through the swamp of applicable codes and regulations for their projects.

- Undertake historic preservation and adaptive reuse.

- Engage with building performance, especially façade design.

- Research on a variety of architecturally related subjects is becoming an interesting and rewarding niche. Materials, envelopes and façades, and other areas in the realm of building science are complemented by studies under the umbrella of social science, such as quantifying the constantly evolving challenges of open office productivity versus that of more traditional layouts.

- Offer expert witness testimony and services in support of resolving design and/or construction disputes.

---

3  For detailed guidance on working effectively with partners in an alliance, see Andrew Pressman, *Designing Relationships: The Art of Collaboration in Architecture*, Abingdon: Routledge, 2014.

Many other services can be packaged together—or separately—to distinguish the Practice. Alternatively, some of the services noted above could be offered independently—with the prospect of an architectural commission in the future. Services related to a fundraising effort for institutional or community buildings are an example: expressing client wishes and dreams through exciting design ideas in the form of three-dimensional architectural renderings with their associated probable costs are much needed for certain client types. Moreover, an architect can serve as a spokesperson and advocate for the project as well as identifying recognition opportunities for donors. So a new fundraising component of the Firm, involving lots of creative design and communication with potential donors, could be dedicated to that service. Architects are indeed *vital* to the success of many capital campaigns, and it is incumbent upon architects to demonstrate how.

With the right alliance, design can be part of a great continuum of services to ensure project success.

*"Escher! Get your ass up here."*

**Figure 7.1**    With the right alliance, design can be part of a great continuum of services to ensure project success.

Robert Leighton/The New Yorker Collection/The Cartoon Bank.

It's important to note that we are *not* talking about more subcontractor work with its anemic 10% markup. We *are* talking about arrangements where the Firm gets additional work for itself with good fees *and* obtains a commission of sorts for its ally for providing the work opportunity; e.g. one-fifth to as much as one-third of the ally's fee. This is a model regularly employed by lawyers, for example. To paraphrase their usual description of shared compensation arrangements: "You eat what you kill, but if someone else drives the kill to you, they get a healthy bite."

2. **Create a niche of specialized services.** Given passion and skill, any one of the services suggested above could potentially be developed into a specialization (or possibly a separate profit center) for the Practice with all of its attendant benefits. Securing a reputation as an expert and as a thought leader could help the Practice market its services locally, nationally, and globally—at the very least, well beyond its current market area.

Here's another example of a niche design service that would especially appeal to Bob: Focused residential design consultations that provide services for schematic design, materials selection, or even an aspect of construction detailing—whatever the overarching idea is toward fulfilling a client's wishes and making poetic, magical space. This could yield a decent profit for the architect, and it is something clients might embrace as well because of the relatively limited scope (and, therefore, fee). There would certainly be a loss of control on the final outcome, but there would be strong design input that would surely influence the project for the better. That concept would direct your Marketing Specialist to focus on a way to publicize within—and outside—the profession.

There are no limits to discovering a unique niche when design thinking is applied to creating an entrepreneurial model that distinguishes a practice with special talent. For example, Mobile Design Studio demonstrates how an innovative design process can result in a niche service.[4] Their approach is to move their studio on-site for various project phases to collaborate more effectively and, ultimately, significantly speed up the process. With new equipment and technology, this is an updated version of the 1950s "squatters" (the Caudill Rowlett Scott term for brainstorming and collaborating on the owner's home turf).

3. **Expand the architectural services pie.** Thomas Fisher has suggested that: "Our clients really should be everybody who owns a building."[5] His argument is that building diagnostics has been a role that architects have relinquished to others; i.e. building or home inspectors (who are typically hired only when there is a sale) or contractors and constructors. Architects are perhaps better suited than anyone to perform this type of work to the highest degrees of excellence given their background in design and construction and their network of industry contacts. Raising this service to professional status could be highly advantageous to both architects and building owners. Catching problems early can

---

4   Erica Malouf, "Real-Time Design," *AIArchitect,* October 10, 2014.
5   Interview with Thomas Fisher, "Models for the Architectural Profession," in Andrew Pressman, *Professional Practice 101: Business Strategies and Case Studies in Architecture*, Hoboken, NJ: Wiley, 2006, pp. 271–276.

save owners lots of money, which can be documented. Analogous to HMOs (health maintenance organizations) in healthcare, architects could create alliances of BMOs (building maintenance organizations) for diagnostics or diagnostics and repair. This would be a recession-proof service since buildings leak, are too hot or too cold, rot and decay, grow mold, and so on, independent of fluctuations in the economy. Taking this a step further, compensation models could be creative as well; i.e. annual premiums. As a function of specific building types, there could be arrangements for periodic building inspections and tune-ups, similar to auto dealerships.

What are some other ways that architectural services can be expanded? Tailor your response and add your own spin by applying creativity and design thinking to forge new entrepreneurial practice models (as in Fisher's example). This could lead to many eureka moments, more work, and more revenue.

4. **Brand new branding.** In the effort to seek a competitive advantage and differentiate the practice, it makes sense for professional service firms to learn from the corporate world and interpret the notion of branding. In this context, branding obviously can be much more than a well-designed logo; it can embody reputation, expertise, design excellence, firm culture, trust, professionalism, aspirations, and so on. The brand is a tangible manifestation of the Firm's mission and vision—its *distinctive* attributes—reflected by completed projects, staff, consultants, and *everyone connected with any related alliance*. It can serve to engender loyalty with clients (who will also refer the Firm to others), acquire new work, and even help to recruit the best talent. Show what it is you do that's so great (perhaps even indispensable) and how you do it. Easier said than done; this—along with the subjects of marketing and business development in depth and detail—are yet more design problems (and subjects for another book). We would add that embracing an entrepreneurial practice model as suggested above will greatly facilitate and drive an effective marketing campaign.

## SMART FEES

Fees are a sensitive issue for architects; this is partly because of two cases[6] against the American Institute of Architects (AIA) for violating the Sherman Antitrust Act, which prohibits monopolies and maintains fair competition. The Justice Department claimed that the AIA was involved in price fixing by providing fee schedules. AIA subsequently entered into consent decrees, effectively not allowing members to directly or indirectly restrain the way architects

---

6  (1) 1972 consent decree between the American Institute of Architects (AIA) and the Department of Justice (DOJ) restricted the AIA from imposing an ethical standard or policy prohibiting members from submitting fee quotations for architectural services. (2) 1990 consent decree between AIA and DOJ directed the AIA and all of its chapters to refrain from adopting any policies, rules, bylaws, or resolutions, or issuing official statements that would restrain AIA members from a) submitting competitive bids or price quotations, including cases where price is the principal consideration in choosing an architect; b) providing discounts; and c) providing free services.

arrive at fees for their services—or even "talk about prices in a way that could be construed as part of a conspiracy to fix prices [which is a] violation of the antitrust laws."[7] As a consequence, there has not been much in the way of critical discourse related to fees, which has not been good for the profession.

As you probably well know, many architects—*those who are members of one of the traditional learned professions that also includes doctors and lawyers*—are not paid as much as plumbers and electricians. There are three characteristics of architects as professionals that suggest this is reprehensible: (1) architects, by virtue of a relatively long and standardized period of education, training, and internship (all of which is regulated by an association of accomplished members of the profession), have mastery of a circumscribed body of material and associated skills; (2) architects are expected to exercise discretion wisely; and (3) architects are expected to accept fiduciary responsibilities at a level well beyond the level expected of tradespeople in the marketplace.[8]

Insufficient fees can obviously result in losing money and/or not having enough time to produce high-quality work. Moreover, architects are renowned for not making as much profit as they should. Why is this so? It is probably due to the two most common ways of arriving at fees:

1. ***Percentage of construction cost.*** This method is a remnant from the distant past. As a consequence, many clients have conventionally budgeted architects' fees as a percentage of construction cost. It is so arbitrary; in many cases, there is little or no relationship between construction cost and design fee. Even if there was a modicum of connection between fee and construction cost, construction costs are quite volatile and vary dramatically by region as a function of labor and material costs. Moreover, percentage of construction cost does not differentiate between the quality and type of services provided by different firms. Often, this method will be used as a check against other methods, which is baffling for the same reasons as noted above. Percentage of construction cost is as outrageous as arriving at a fee solely based on time and overhead expenses, as elaborated below.

2. ***Time plus overhead costs.*** Starting with a project schedule, various iterations of specific tasks, staff who will be working on those tasks, and time projections can be detailed and compared. Multiplying the total hours by a designated average hourly rate (or by a rate for each staff person) will yield the fee. Overhead costs are built into the hourly rate. Exhibits 7.1 and 7.2 show an example of task budgets and a summary for all project phases for a renovation of a private school for which Mary was the Partner-in-Charge and Zuda was the Project Manager with Richard and Frank completing the internal design team. Exhibit 7.3 shows the total fee for this project, including consultants.

---

7  Jay A. Stephens, Hon. AIA, Senior Vice President and general counsel of the AIA, in Elizabeth Evitts Dickinson, "A Better Value," *Architect*, January 2014, p. 113.

8  Carl M. Sapers, "Professionalism and the Public Interest," in Andrew Pressman, *Professional Practice 101: Business Strategies and Case Studies in Architecture*, Hoboken, NJ: Wiley, 2006, p. 5.

(NB: The tasks in the Task Budget example [Exhibit 7.1] are conventional; they represent a two-dimensional work plan for conventional services rather than those of a three-dimensional modeling process [i.e. BIM]. But the principles are similar: identify the tasks and then the personnel and time required to execute them. It may be more of a challenge to quantify collaboration time but the more fine-tuning of task descriptions in this environment, the better the idea of actual time needed to complete them.)

**EXHIBIT 7.1** Task Budget

| TASK DESCRIPTION | STAFF HOURS | | | | TOTAL HOURS | GROSS COST ($) |
| --- | --- | --- | --- | --- | --- | --- |
| | MM | ZO | RW | FB | | |
| **PRE-DESIGN** | | | | | | |
| Field Survey | | 4 | | 4 | 8 | 800 |
| Prepare Base Drawings | | 4 | | 8 | 12 | 1,200 |
| User Program Meeting | | 4 | 4 | | 8 | 800 |
| SUBTOTAL PRE-DESIGN | 0 | 12 | 4 | 12 | 28 | **2,800** |
| **SCHEMATIC DESIGN** | | | | | | |
| Develop/Confirm Plan, Elevations | 1 | 6 | 20 | 6 | 33 | 3,300 |
| User Review Meeting | | 6 | 4 | | 10 | 1,000 |
| Research Lab Equipment | | 4 | 2 | | 6 | 600 |
| Finishes Selections | 2 | | 8 | 12 | 22 | 2,200 |
| Presentation | 2 | | 12 | 12 | 26 | 2,600 |
| Meeting Minutes/Administration | | 14 | 8 | | 22 | 2,200 |
| SUBTOTAL SCHEMATIC DESIGN | 5 | 30 | 54 | 30 | 119 | **11,900** |
| **DESIGN DEVELOPMENT** | | | | | | |
| Outline Specifications | 1 | 6 | 2 | | 9 | 900 |
| Engineering Backgrounds | | | | 6 | 6 | 600 |
| Engineering Meeting/Walkthrough | | 6 | | | 6 | 600 |
| Develop Special Details | | 24 | 12 | 6 | 42 | 4,200 |
| Lab Lighting Design/Ceilings | 1 | 6 | | 6 | 13 | 1,300 |
| Research Code Issues | | 8 | | | 8 | 800 |
| Meeting Minutes/Administration | 1 | 16 | 4 | | 21 | 2,100 |
| SUBTOTAL DESIGN DEVELOPMENT | 3 | 66 | 18 | 18 | 105 | **10,500** |
| **CONSTRUCTION DOCUMENTS** | | | | | | |
| (2) Construction Floor and Ceiling Plans | | 16 | | 16 | 32 | 3,200 |
| (1½) Elevation Drawings | | 6 | | 8 | 14 | 1,400 |
| (1) Detail Sheet/Typical | | 8 | 2 | 16 | 26 | 2,600 |
| (1) Detail Sheet/Skylight and Roof | | 12 | 2 | 2 | 16 | 1,600 |
| Finishes Coordination | | 6 | 2 | 16 | 24 | 2,400 |
| (1) Symbols/Schedules/Notes | | 8 | 4 | 8 | 20 | 2,000 |
| Landmarks Submission | | 4 | | | 4 | 400 |
| Building Department Submission | | 8 | | 12 | 20 | 2,000 |
| Specifications | | 30 | 6 | 10 | 46 | 4,600 |
| Coordination/Consultants | | 8 | 1 | 4 | 13 | 1,300 |
| Meeting Minutes/Administration | 1 | 8 | 1 | | 10 | 1,000 |
| SUBTOTAL CONSTRUCTION DOCUMENTS | 1 | 114 | 18 | 92 | 225 | **22,500** |

**EXHIBIT 7.1** *continued*

| TASK DESCRIPTION | STAFF HOURS | | | | TOTAL HOURS | GROSS COST ($) |
|---|---|---|---|---|---|---|
| | MM | ZO | RW | FB | | |
| **BID PHASE** | | | | | | |
| Documents and Notices Distribution | | 3 | | 5 | 8 | 800 |
| Attend Pre-Bid Meeting | | 4 | | 2 | 6 | 600 |
| Clarifications/Addenda | | 8 | | 14 | 22 | 2,200 |
| Review Bids/Recommend | 3 | 12 | | 3 | 18 | 1,800 |
| SUBTOTAL BID PHASE | 3 | 27 | 0 | 24 | 54 | **5,400** |
| **PRE-CONSTRUCTION ADMINISTRATION** | | | | | | |
| Site Visits/Meetings/Minutes | | 12 | | | 12 | 1,200 |
| Shop Drawing Review | | 50 | 4 | 2 | 56 | 5,600 |
| SUBTOTAL PRE-CONSTRUCTION ADMIN. | 0 | 62 | 4 | 2 | 68 | **6,800** |
| **CONSTRUCTION ADMINISTRATION** | | | | | | |
| Site Visits/Meetings/Minutes | | 34 | | | 34 | 3,400 |
| Shop Drawing Review | | 20 | 2 | 2 | 24 | 2,400 |
| Punch List | | 10 | | | 10 | 1,000 |
| SUBTOTAL CONSTRUCTION ADMIN. | 0 | 64 | 2 | 2 | 68 | **6,800** |
| GRAND TOTAL | **12** | **375** | **100** | **180** | **667** | **66,700** |
| Assumed Average Rate Per Hour | | | | | | $100 |

**EXHIBIT 7.2** Task Budget Summary by Project Phase

| TASK DESCRIPTION | STAFF HOURS | | | | TOTAL HOURS | GROSS COST ($) | % OF TOTAL |
|---|---|---|---|---|---|---|---|
| | MM | ZO | RW | FB | | | |
| **SUMMARY** | | | | | | | |
| Pre-design | 0 | 12 | 4 | 12 | 28 | 2,800 | 4.0 |
| Schematic Design | 5 | 30 | 54 | 30 | 119 | 11,900 | 17.5 |
| Design Development | 3 | 66 | 18 | 18 | 105 | 10,500 | 15.7 |
| Construction Documents | 1 | 114 | 18 | 92 | 225 | 22,500 | 33.7 |
| Bid Phase | 3 | 27 | 0 | 24 | 54 | 5,400 | 8.1 |
| Pre-construction | 0 | 62 | 4 | 2 | 68 | 6,800 | 10.5 |
| Construction Administration | 0 | 64 | 2 | 2 | 68 | 6,800 | 10.5 |
| TOTAL LABOR | **12** | **375** | **100** | **180** | **667** | **66,700** | **100.0** |
| Assumed Average Rate Per Hour | | | | | | 100 | |

**EXHIBIT 7.3** Total Fee Including Consultants

| | $ | % |
|---|---|---|
| **Total Labor** | **66,700** | **87.0** |
| **CONSULTANTS** | | |
| Mechanical, Electrical, Plumbing | 7,000 | 9.1 |
| Structural | 1,500 | 2.0 |
| Expediter | 1,000 | 1.3 |
| TOTAL CONSULTANTS | **9,500** | **12.4** |
| Direct Expenses | 500 | 0.6 |
| **TOTAL COST/FEE** | **76,700** | **100.0** |
| | | |
| Estimated Construction Cost | $756,600 | |
| FEE % OF CONSTRUCTION COST | 10.1% | |

Richard Watson (recall the iconoclastic, arrogant, yet experienced staffer from Chapter 2) suggested modifying the program for the School to include adult education classes in the evenings utilizing several existing classrooms. Part of the proposal was to have the ability to close down the rest of the facility (except for toilets) when evening classes were in session. This idea was fully embraced by the School administration as it would provide a significant new and much-needed income stream. Does this idea have more tangible value to the client than a mere straightforward upgrading of space? Yes! Is it worth more to the client than the architect's time? Yes!

Can M&B architects learn from this when setting the fee for their next school project? Hoping so—especially if they provide the evidence of value and document the additional annual revenue for the School as a result of their design services. In circumstances in which precise savings to or additional revenue for the client will be unknown until the problem is engaged, the fee can be partially open-ended; i.e. the fee will be increased by x if the design's outcome is y. This approach will ensure that the Firm remains competitive with regard to fee.

Occasionally, time is sold at a higher rate or a lower rate—depending on what the market will bear and what the client expects to pay for a particular project. The true earned rate will vary materially if the architect's perception of the effort required for the project turns out to be underestimated or overstated. As New York architect Norman Rosenfeld, FAIA, said: "It's not a science; it's an art with a little bit of science mixed into it." It is important to anticipate which clients are indecisive, or who, for other reasons, will require time-intensive handholding, and to build that into the fee. Still, this is not the best way to set a fee.

For projects beginning with an ill-defined scope of work, time might be an appropriate way to begin the fee negotiation, at least for the preliminary work to get an understanding of the project and pin down the scope. Likewise, during the latter stages of a project where the constructor is not performing well, additional fees may be required to cover the costs of more field visits and construction administration.

All this is not to suggest that time is unimportant. On the contrary, it is critical to know the actual cost of doing the work so that appropriate profit can be determined and to monitor progress in terms of time and fee as explained in previous chapters. This will enable problems to be discovered early and corrections to be implemented.

Still, one protection to build into contracts is to permit additional fees to be charged if more time is required because of unforeseen delays by the client or others on the job. That's not an easy sell; but it is much easier if the deal is structured so that time savings are shared through a credit toward fees, but with the calculation of that credit yielding some bonus to the architect for the savings. If the architect is getting a portion of the fee for time that is *not* worked, the effect is to raise the overall rate of pay for time that *is* worked. As long as there is enough work toward filling capacity and the time is profitably used elsewhere, the Firm benefits and its offer of a possible credit becomes a selling point.

## Fees Based on Time and Value

Perhaps the most rational and fair way of setting fees is time plus value. Value can be defined in a number of ways. First and foremost, the value of professional services is much more than time and overhead costs: it is creative and technical expertise supported by experience, education, and professional judgment—all applied to the client's specific project. Architects should not sell *time* by itself; rather, they should sell their *professional services*. The notion that architects are just selling time doesn't make sense—or enough profit—for a professional in today's society.

While it certainly is not easy to quantify the value of "magic" in great architectural design, there are some ways to quantify design excellence and benefit to clients. Some examples follow:

▪ A brilliant idea for schematic design will dramatically reduce staffing costs for a client. If the architect can eliminate one full-time employee in running a facility, that could amount to a savings of $50,000/year or $1 million over 20 years. That can certainly justify a fee that greatly exceeds the time expended developing the design, even though it might require a lot of professional time to understand the client's operations and then propose a bold design idea to achieve those savings. Familiarity with a particular industry, however, may rapidly lead to that client-customized understanding.

▪ Another example of significant value-added service is to quantify energy, water, janitorial, and other building services savings as a function of the architectural design.

▪ "Substantial" residential renovations account for an average 60% return for homeowners.[9]

---

9   Fisher Thomas, "Value Added," *Architect*, March 2014, p. 66.

- Getting donors on board for a capital campaign with renderings of a stunning building and persuasive presentations is an irrefutably valuable service.

- Efficient space planning combined with careful scheduling of multipurpose rooms could reduce required square footage, resulting in considerable and documentable savings.

- Your access to or participation in a unique set of alliances that allow you to provide a spectrum of valuable services will set you apart from other practices and justify higher fees, as would your expertise in providing a specialized service.

Another avenue that might be worth investigating is partnering with a client/developer to become financially invested in a project. A percentage of the fee (not the entire fee) could be exchanged for an equity stake in the client's enterprise. As with any real estate investing, however, there are associated risks that need to be identified and carefully considered in addition to potential gain. However, this is not an idea that would make sense when a firm is strained for cash or low on reserves. Beware too that depending on the structure of such an arrangement, liabilities may also be actually or contingently shared with the corresponding effect of counting against borrowing capacity.

Ostensibly, fee should not be the *primary* consideration for a client to select an architect. If it is then the architect is not doing a good enough job—or being creative enough—in clearly articulating the value of a firm's services. Or the architect is chasing the wrong client.

## BACKLOG MANAGEMENT

Another factor that may influence fee levels is the size of the Practice's backlog. It should— but not from a purely emotional standpoint of whether the Principals and staff are feeling overworked, hungry (or even desperate) for work, or somewhere in between.

The reason backlog management is important is that the level of demand on the Firm's resources impacts costs. If overtime is needed from hourly employees, their costs go up by 50%. If overtime at some other rate is contractually promised to professionals, that's an additional cost. Error rates are statistically higher when workers are under pressure because of a heavy workload. Large backlogs suggest that times are flush and less care is usually taken to conserve resources and costs.

And when backlogs are low, fees may be lowered. Less creditworthy clients may be accepted (a problem that seems to have seriously infected and affected Michelangelo & Brunelleschi). Standards for projects may be lowered, diffusing focus.

There are two keys to wise backlog management.

As it is with so many of the problems we've examined, one key is having up-to-date data, especially data regarding cash flow (current and projected), and forward-looking scheduling. Both of these subjects have been discussed at length, but it's worth noting that in the final analysis, managers must manage a firm's resources.

Cash is the common denominator for all those resources and must be available at all times to cover the costs of operating. That's the most fundamental business management responsibility.

Management of staff, for which scheduling is the primary tool, obviously requires matching staff to projects so the work can be performed. Scheduling should include modeling how the backlog will be accomplished into the future. The scheduler should be looking far into the future, exchanging information regularly with those marketing, considering the staff time "what-ifs" of receiving this or that contract (especially relatively large ones), and building in contingency plans to deal with emergencies—and opportunities.

If backlog is high and schedules are becoming crowded, the temptation to charge more for the higher demand should arise. Conversely, if schedules are open, the temptation may also arise to reduce fees to fill the void.

That's where the other key comes in—being in touch with the market. All declines must tautologically be preceded by a high point; all upsurges by a nadir. Calling the turns and relating those to the circumstances of the Firm, including in particular its backlog and current fee structure, is where management judgment—call it management intuition if you will—is indispensable. While some individuals have a greater sixth sense for this art than others, frequent, if not constant, attention to the marketplace and its data will improve the odds that the wisest decisions can be made and temptation embraced or rejected. Moreover, if embraced, the degree to which the temptation is indulged is more likely to be wisely calibrated.

As an aside, it's worth recognizing that managing those resources means looking into the future, setting expectations, making predictions, and wisely deploying resources accordingly. That takes time and it takes it away from actually doing design, presumably the first love of a design professional.

For M&B, that implies that Bob is rendering a valuable service by sacrificing significant time to management, *assuming* his decisions are wise and his performance is good. But if Bob's heart is not in that effort or if those assumptions are misplaced to any significant degree, an alternative may be to look at hiring a Business Manager. The analysis for that possible position would involve the same process as for the Marketing Specialist. In fact, perhaps that means M&B should be considering someone for a position of Business Manager instead of a Marketing Specialist because it seems certain that, at the present, the Firm cannot afford both. A Business Manager's job will encompass marketing duties, though that's just a part of the portfolio and almost certainly a minority part. Just maybe, that part-time effort is all the Firm needs right now. M&B's backlog, current prospects, and the likely higher cost for a Business Manager are all material to the question *if* Bob and Mary want to consider this aside.

## TEACHING, LECTURING, AND WRITING

Many issues of professional practice are interconnected and overlapping such as practice specialties, business development, and recruiting talent. Dissemination of your work and communication about what differentiates the practice are important for just about everyone. A strategy that can be leveraged across media and in support of reinforcing brand (as described above) is to get exposure to various audiences and constituencies by teaching, lecturing, and writing. Take advantage of all possible venues for speaking and teaching; i.e. AIA professional development conferences, universities, business groups including the local Chamber of Commerce, and other organizations that have prospective and current clients as members.

Identifying where your writing should be placed for maximum impact, exposure, and dissemination is part of the ongoing design problem. The content will help to differentiate the firm, attract new clients, and reinforce your niche with existing clients.

A whole series of focused public relations strategies goes hand in hand with maintaining a reputation as an expert, including writing in both peer-reviewed and client-read publications, whether it's *Architectural Digest* or just the city's monthly focus magazine and/or developing an online newsletter or blog for building lessors, operators, and Realtors on the commercial side and/or homeowner and condominium association officers and board members on the residential side. These and other assignments should be a part of the job description for the new Marketing Specialist. That job description should also include researching to find the organizations where M&B should be recognized and making the contacts to initiate that process.

Active participation in teaching or conducting seminars, lecturing, and writing will bolster professional credibility, help in the search for talent, and transform you into a recognized thought leader and go-to person for the media in your area of specialization. Moreover, if these activities become ingrained in Firm culture then that leaves the door open for serendipity and luck to strike early and often.

## PRO BONO WORK

Pro bono work—providing services for the public good to those people or groups who might not otherwise afford architectural services—should be an integral component of Practice culture (and *any* business model) for multiple reasons. First and foremost, it's a fundamentally noble thing to do and part of an architect's professional responsibilities. Even the AIA *2012 Code of Ethics and Professional Conduct*, Canon II, states that members "should promote and serve the public interest in their personal and professional activities." Pro bono work can be inherently satisfying, meaningful, and something that you can feel passionate about. There are secondary benefits to engaging in pro bono work as well that include the following:

- Acquiring experience in project types and/or services that may be new to you will enhance your portfolio.

- The exposure, contacts, and potential public relations that result may produce leads for future work.

- Engaging in this type of work may help to recruit the best talent.

- Leadership and learning opportunities will be available for young staff.

The important point is to keep your eyes open for worthy local projects to which you can contribute your special skills and energy.

And here is a related, albeit very different, message. If you—and everyone in the Practice—is coached and incentivized to adopt this culture of doing good for others, it can be applied on a regular basis to contacts in your current professional network. Offering opinions, clipping articles, forwarding links, etc. that might provide some specific assistance has the potential, over time, to yield new business. Every contact for each staff member should be considered valuable and a prospective referral source to nurture. (See Chapter 8 for more discussion on this aspect of firm culture.)

## WORK PLANNING TO REDUCE COSTS AND INCREASE EFFICIENCY

1. *The virtual/physical office hybrid.* The idea of working out of your spare bedroom in your pajamas with a laptop and high-speed Internet connection has a certain appeal from an overhead perspective not to mention a greatly reduced morning commute. But seriously, a virtual office that has flexibility to expand, downsize, and create alliances by electronically linking the consultants and key staff—all as a function of specific projects— holds a strategic attractiveness. Participants can indeed be located anywhere in the world (subject to proper compliance with any applicable licensing, regulatory, and taxa- tion requirements). That could even be considered another form of outsourcing, perhaps with more control.

   The other extreme, the physical office, provides the context for the all-important face-to- face meetings that are the necessary prerequisite to any subsequent virtual meetings, ensuring the latter will be optimally productive. It is conventional wisdom and human nature that personal rapport is essential to building and maintaining respect and effective working relationships.

   Consider a hybrid of the virtual and the physical to create an idealized workplace in which face time is critical but so is working independently. A downsized physical office can sig- nificantly reduce overhead but can also provide space for collaboration, client meetings, and so on. Taking this a step further, the physical office could even be situated in a tem- porary space contingent upon the location of projects, consultants, and staff. However, the impact on reputation or image of *not* having a permanent or identified headquarters must be considered.

2. ***Shared space and staff.*** Another model to examine is shared space and even shared staff among one or more other practices to greatly reduce overhead. The space itself, in addition to some support personnel such as a receptionist, could be shared. Furthermore, the skilled workforce could divide full-time work into part-time for multiple firms in the same space. Scheduling, insurance, liability indemnities, benefit plan coordination, and other legal issues arise when considering such arrangements. A practical solution, which may also improve the Firm's balance sheet, is to establish a new entity, jointly owned with the other participating practices, which has the responsibility for the shared space, equipment, and personnel, and charges out at agreed rates for usage. The arrangements for management and control—right down to hiring and firing decisions for that receptionist, for example—must be thoughtfully worked out. Good personal chemistry and trust is essential among the professional participants, but this can be a way to materially reduce overhead without sacrificing resource availability and performance quality.

Consider all the above work planning factors as another element that can inform the brainstorming of alternate new business models for your Practice.

## RESOURCE INVESTMENT

A discussion of the workplace—whether physical, virtual, or some combination thereof—leads to the question of how to use resources effectively and for maximum return on investment. Renting office space is an expense with no return; sharing office space, as noted above, can reduce overhead but is still a drain. Owning the space and/or the building in which it resides, on the other hand, might be an excellent investment. Consider this as a real estate investment project. *Designing* the building, the workspace, or even some of the components within it, such as the furniture, can be beneficial in multiple ways. The design—a three-dimensional, tangible expression of the Firm's core mission and values—can be leveraged for awards, publicity, and prospective client education about the Practice, Principals, and staff.

If adequate cash is available for purchase, the ideal situation is one in which the cash flow costs of carrying the property are less than the alternative cost of renting. Those carrying costs include mortgage, insurance, taxes, utilities, maintenance, and repairs.

The Firm's Principals can use a building as a way to build wealth by putting the property into a separate entity (usually an LLC is desired) and having the Firm pay rent to that entity. Under current law and for a long time, that arrangement has offered certain tax advantages. Financially, it tends to improve liquidity and borrowing power and to support clearer accounting. Those advantages are in addition to the legal advantage of insulating liability. That's on top of the assurance that the building's owner is not going to make decisions about the building that are negative for the Practice.

So, the two questions for Bob and Mary are:

1. Would an owned building be financially superior to renting?

2. If so, can they afford the investment that a purchase will require?

To examine that decision for M&B, we need some specs for such a building. Briefly:

- With the two additional employees (Marketing Specialist and second Administrator) the staff is up to 12 people. To work from a baseline, Mary and Bob determine they want at least enough space to handle a 25% increase in staff; so that would be 15 people. At a rough standard of 200 square feet per person, that's a minimum of 3,000 square feet.

- Bob and Mary envision a two-story commercial, slab foundation building, which will permit a smaller lot size and yield a marginally less expensive building cost per square foot.

- With 3,000 square feet, research shows that the average building cost per square foot in their suburban market, exclusive of land, is $200. Accordingly, building cost should come in at about $600,000.

- The generally accepted Floor Area Ratio in their metropolitan area under the zoning regulations of the various suburban municipalities is 1.0, meaning that the lot size would also have to be at least 3,000 square feet.

- However, with the municipal parking requirements and green space that Mary and Bob feel is essential to convey the right image for the Practice, they calculate they need a lot of roughly 4,000 square feet.

- Review of Web sites suggests that the cost for a buildable commercial lot within the acceptable area would cost around $150,000.

- Together, those two pieces (lot purchase and construction costs) yield a total project cost of $150,000 + $600,000 = $750,000.

Very possibly the showstopper for Mary and Bob is the initial cash to fund the project. Their banker confirms financing would be available (initially as a construction loan to be replaced by a take-out commercial mortgage) for 75% of the project value, which means cash of $187,500 would be needed. In order to have a reasonable contingency fund available, they need to plan on having $200,000 available. A glance at the balance sheet makes clear that's a non-starter in the Firm's current condition.

But Bob and Mary each have the necessary personal funds and that presents a second option, which is favored by most legal advisors. That option would be to establish a separate entity (most commonly a limited liability company taxed as a partnership) to buy the lot, build the facility, and lease it back to the Firm on a triple net basis (i.e. with the Firm paying all operating costs as part of the lease term).

The oft-cited legal advantages are:

- Separating and insulating[10] this valuable asset from the general operating liabilities the Practice faces.[11]

- With two entities, the investment to operate the Practice becomes more liquid. For example, the Firm (or one Principal's interest) might be sold or the Firm merged with another while the realty was retained as an asset.

- Tax advantages[12] are likely to accrue, both while operating and upon any disposition of the property.

- Opportunities for obtainment of additional credit may well be greater with two entities than with one; i.e. the sum of the parts may be greater than the whole.

- Additional investors in the real estate can be brought in, if desired, without any legal right to involvement in the business. For professional entities in which ownership may be limited, partially or entirely to licensees, this may be an important factor. Bob and Mary agree to have their spouses, Sally and Jim, as co-owners so that each of the two shares will be owned jointly by each married couple.[13]

- The marital ownership highlights the additional advantage of improving estate planning. In this case, while Mary and Bob will have a Buy-Sell Agreement[14] for the Practice, as an additional recommendation from Sloan & Wharton, the property interest in the LLC need not necessarily be bought out as the possibility for continued rental income to a surviving spouse may be attractive. Furthermore, the flexibility of such an arrangement is also a plus if the event occurs at a time that would make a transaction difficult to accomplish or otherwise disadvantageous.

- The flip side of the ownership advantages for the real estate entity is the ability to bring in owners to the Practice without the real estate being involved. So, for example, if Bob and Mary want to offer ownership down the line to one or more staffers, ignoring the value of the real estate for such purposes makes such transactions easier. If the arrangement is a

---

10  Such insulation is not absolute, especially if Mary and/or Bob were tagged with malpractice liability, but it substantially reduces the risk that the property could be liened or seized by creditors—whether tort, governmental, or contract creditors—of the Firm.

11  Of course, it's a virtual certainty that the lender will require personal guarantees from Mary and Bob and maybe from their spouses as well.

12  Discussion of those advantages is beyond the scope of this book and will likely vary to a lesser or greater extent by location. However, they can be a major factor in any decision.

13  Spousal ownership will assure that the spouses also will have to be guarantors, a factor to be considered if otherwise avoidable.

14  A Buy-Sell Agreement between them provides for the buyout of one Principal's interest if certain events occur—death, disability, delicensing, disappearance, incarceration, bankruptcy (and, possibly, retirement, expulsion [when there are more than two or disproportionate ownerships], and voluntary withdrawal). Such agreements often include life insurance, which can further serve as a source of savings and/or as a retirement benefit.

buy-in to any extent, the value to be paid for is presumably going to be lower (assuming the value of the real estate does not end up under water), but if the transfer is additional compensation to the employee then the lower value reduces the tax hit for the employee and the employment tax and other payroll overhead costs (those that are based on total compensation; i.e. worker compensation and comprehensive liability insurances) for the Firm. Additionally, the psychological barrier for Bob and Mary of what they would be giving up in taking the dramatic step of adding a Principal, whether an employee or an outsider, is lowered because the value involved is correspondingly less. On the other hand, they also can agree (here's more flexibility) to include a Principal as an owner in the real estate entity; an example of the liquidity advantage referenced above and, possibly, invoking some tax advantages.

Contrapuntally, there are some disadvantages, most notably the costs of establishing the separate entity, maintaining two sets of books and bank accounts, filing two sets of tax returns (federal and state and possibly municipal), and performing the other duties attendant to maintaining an entity in good legal standing. Some commentators also point to the potential for conflicts in goals between the two entities, which is a much higher risk where there is not an identity of ownership between the entities; as the inclusion here of spouses in the real estate entity may portend. Another potential source of conflict for M&B relates to the new compensation plan as manipulating rent will affect profits, a key factor on which incentive compensation for staff will be based. If staff comes to believe that rent is being unfairly charged,[15] that could be a source of serious discontent.[16]

With the recommendation of Wharton and Sloan, as well as their attorney and CPA, the idea of a separate entity is indeed desirable; and with spousal support, both can put in the necessary $100,000 so the cash investment is not going to be a showstopper after all. But is such a decision wise in and of itself, assuming a buildable lot in a desirable location can be found and the other pieces, especially the bank financing, can be put in place?

The starting point for the analysis is the current rent that is being paid. In Chapter 6, the rent was described as rising to $60,267 for the coming year, but that figure only covered an increase for additional space for just three-quarters of the year so the increase of $9,387 shown in Exhibit 6.7 needs to be normalized:

Annualized Increase: $9,367 \times (4/3) = $12,489
Normalized Annual Cost: $50,880 + $12,489 = $63,369

---

15  Rents that are outside the range of fair market rents may also have untoward tax consequences if challenged by tax authorities, strongly suggesting that reasonable rents should be adhered to as a mantra of dual related entities.

16  The circumstances of any particular firm, whether owned by one or more persons, may offer additional advantages (reflective of the greater flexibility usually available from a separate real estate entity) or may result in disadvantages. Assistance from an attorney and a tax advisor is enjoined in considering the option.

Similarly, utilities also need to be normalized:

Annualized Increase: $1,375 \times (4/3) = $1,833
Normalized Annual Cost: $11,208 + $1,833 = $13,041

Hence, the total starting point metric to test against projected costs for a proprietary property is:

Rent + Utilities = $63,369 + $13,041 = $76,041/year

It's important to recognize that the rent is due to automatically increase by 3% per year, and it's fair to expect a similar rate of inflation for the utilities. As it'll take about a year to get a property ready for occupancy, the actual cost for the first year of comparison will need to be inflated accordingly.

The one other expense incurred currently as tenant is for a tenant's insurance policy, which is projected to be $1,200 per year beginning one year away.

To develop the figures for comparison, the assumptions for the financing are for a 25-year loan with a 5% interest rate. Consequently, the annual cash flow comparison will be derived from the figures in Exhibit 7.4.

A significant saving is expected in utilities with some of the design features Bob and Mary have in mind, which will compare very favorably to the 20-year-old building in which they are currently leasing. They also project that they should not see an increase in repair costs in a brand new structure until after the third year. They recognize they will now have maintenance,

**EXHIBIT 7.4** Annual Costs Profile: Rent v. Own

| CASH FLOW | Base Cost ($) | Annual Adjustment |
|---|---|---|
| *PURCHASE ALTERNATIVE* | | |
| Mortgage Payment | 39,460 | Fixed |
| Real Estate Taxes | 6,000 | 2.5% Inflation |
| Insurance | 1,500 | 2% Inflation |
| Utilities | 7,200 | 3% Inflation |
| Maintenance, Janitorial & Trash | 6,000 | 3% Inflation |
| Repairs/Replacement Reserve | 6,000 | 0% 1st 3 years, then 3% |
| Security Monitoring | 600 | 3% Inflation |
| | | |
| *RENT ALTERNATIVE* | | |
| Rent (Incl. Common Area Costs) | 63,369 | 3% Inflation |
| Insurance | 1,200 | 2% Inflation |
| Utilities | 13,041 | 3% Inflation |

**EXHIBIT 7.5** Cash Flow Comparison: Rent v. Own

| RENT | Year 1 | Year 2 | Year 3 | Year 4 | Year 5 | Year 6 | Year 7 | Cumulated |
|---|---|---|---|---|---|---|---|---|
| Rent (Incl. CA Costs) | 63,369 | 65,270 | 67,228 | 69,245 | 71,322 | 73,462 | 75,666 | 485,563 |
| Insurance | 1,200 | 1,224 | 1,248 | 1,273 | 1,299 | 1,325 | 1,351 | 8,921 |
| Utilities | 13,041 | 13,432 | 13,835 | 14,250 | 14,678 | 15,118 | 15,572 | 99,926 |
| Totals | 64,569 | 66,494 | 68,477 | 70,518 | 72,621 | 74,787 | 77,017 | 494,484 |

| PURCHASE | | | | | | | | |
|---|---|---|---|---|---|---|---|---|
| Mortgage Payment | 39,460 | 39,460 | 39,460 | 39,460 | 39,460 | 39,460 | 39,460 | 276,219 |
| Real Estate Taxes | 6,000 | 6,150 | 6,304 | 6,461 | 6,623 | 6,788 | 6,958 | 45,285 |
| Insurance | 1,500 | 1,530 | 1,561 | 1,592 | 1,624 | 1,656 | 1,689 | 11,151 |
| Utilities | 8,400 | 8,652 | 8,912 | 9,179 | 9,454 | 9,738 | 10,030 | 64,365 |
| Maint., Janit. & Trash | 6,000 | 6,180 | 6,365 | 6,556 | 6,753 | 6,956 | 7,164 | 45,975 |
| Repairs/Replace. Res. | 6,000 | 6,000 | 6,000 | 6,180 | 6,365 | 6,556 | 6,753 | 43,855 |
| Security Monitoring | 600 | 618 | 637 | 656 | 675 | 696 | 716 | 4,597 |
| Annual LLC Costs | 2,000 | 1,000 | 1,030 | 1,061 | 1,093 | 1,126 | 1,159 | 8,468 |
| Totals | 69,960 | 69,590 | 70,268 | 71,145 | 72,047 | 72,975 | 73,930 | 499,915 |
| Net Pretax Effect | −5,391 | −3,096 | −1,791 | −626 | 574 | 1,812 | 3,087 | −5,431 |

security costs, and taxes to pay that are subsumed in the common area (CA) costs they are currently paying.

Mary and Bob expect that such a building should (conservatively) be good for seven years before it is outgrown. They actually expect and hope to grow faster but believe that they will have some flexibility to expand staff to beyond 15 and will be able to house as many as 20 comfortably. Plus they hope to take advantage of the trend toward remote working, which they believe will further reduce space pressure. Additionally, with their lot size, they have room to increase parking if needed, and they've agreed to look for a site convenient to public transportation to hopefully further reduce parking pressures.

With those assumptions in mind, they first figure the net savings on a pretax cash flow basis (see Exhibit 7.5):

Not so remarkably, the net pretax effect over seven years averages less than $1,000 per year. But the after-tax effects for the Principals are important. Assuming both couples are in a combined federal and state net tax bracket of 32%, the after-tax result is shown in Exhibit 7.6.

Those numbers are somewhat comforting, although over those seven years with the fact that it's unlikely the assumptions will pan out exactly as assumed, practically speaking, these results are a wash. But what happens at the end of seven years?

In all probability they'd sell the property, which would hopefully give them a nice gain or at least recovery of their investment, including the principal amortized by mortgage payments; but assuming Mary and Bob will be staying in practice, that money would need to be reinvested in a replacement property. Yes, when the Principals are ready to sell out or retire,

**EXHIBIT 7.6** After-Tax Analysis: Rent v. Own

| Deductions: | |
|---|---:|
| Net Deductible Losses | 5,431 |
| Non-deductible Mortgage Payments | −94,768 |
| Capitalized Organization Costs | −2,000 |
| Addback Depreciation | 142,373 |
| Addback Organization Costs Amortization | 933 |
| Total Net Deductions | 51,969 |
| Times Tax Rate | 32% |
| Tax Savings in Cash | 16,630 |

| RECAP: | |
|---|---:|
| Net Cash Losses | −5,431 |
| Tax Savings in Cash | 16,630 |
| Net Cash Benefit | **11,199** |

there may be a nice nest egg available to them; and assumptions could be made about a growth rate in value, which has, of course, been the long-term trend for real estate—though not risk-free, not universally, and not necessarily when evaluated between any two points in time, which are the unavoidably discrete purchase and disposition determinants for gain.

The analysis also does not consider the opportunity cost of the $200,000 invested, which would presumably be earning a return through interest or the like over those seven years. So, in fact, the net effect on the owners might be marginally negative, depending on what rate of return is assumed. Furthermore, the analysis could be made more sophisticated by calculating the present value of all the financial pieces, assuming an implicit discount rate or making calculations year to year (or even in more frequent periods) with assumptions about changes in discount rate. Similarly, models could be run with differing inflation rates for the costs and rents.

But it seems safe to assume that such an effort is not going to vary the final outcome by so much around this best estimate case as to make the decision a slam dunk. Fundamentally, this looks like a wash; so what that suggests is that the subjective factors (which could also be quantified and factored into the analysis as benefits and costs) are the issues on which the final decision will be made.

*Benefits* include:

■ total custom design of the space from the ground up;

■ independence from landlord restrictions;

■ reduction in uncertainty;

■ improvement in image, translating into more and better clients and projects;

■ increase in long-term wealth.

*Costs* include:

■ time requirements for acquisition and construction;

■ more time for facilities management;

■ tied to one location.

Bob and Mary have arranged a Firm-wide strategic planning session to critically assess the direction of the Practice, including input on owning versus renting, and then to develop ideas for an appropriate new business model in response to their professional goals and profit targets.

# 8

## PROGRESS NOTES: WRAPPING UP AND MOVING FORWARD

*I'm interested in seeing design professionals survive because I believe, with a little bit of help, you can change the world—or at least the corner of it where you practice.*

—**Rosslyn F. Foote**[1]

"**W**e are on the way to becoming a well-oiled machine! We're humming along!" exclaimed Bob. "Thanks to Sloan and Wharton—and of course, our and the staff's investment in the process—we have a new strategic plan in place, which is not sitting on the shelf getting dusty."

1 Rosslyn F. Foote, *Running an Office for Fun and Profit: Business Techniques for Small Design Firms,* Stroudsburg, PA: Dowden, Hutchinson & Ross, 1978, p. 106.

"I agree," said Mary. "I'm excited about applying design thinking across the board, from building on our traditional projects to interesting new consulting work, to our constantly evolving business plan. And to think it all started with that Caribbean retreat; there's something magical about the tropics that nurtures life, inspires reflection, and enables growth on many dimensions."

## STAFF INVOLVEMENT WITH CLIENTS, ADMINISTRATION, AND BUSINESS DEVELOPMENT

### Rotating Administrative Roles

Sloan highlighted one of the lessons arising from the recent Firm-wide strategic planning session that Mary and Bob can immediately operationalize: empower the employees, and take full advantage of their passions and untapped abilities. Cultivating leadership from the ranks by rotating administrative roles[2] among senior staff or project managers, for example, has multiple benefits. Aside from keeping staff happy, challenged, and growing professionally, this idea creates opportunities for staff to understand the nuances of running a practice—as well as its totality—and then also to contribute to running it, thus relieving the principals from some of that responsibility. Every employee can be valuable beyond a specific task they're assigned to if they have the broader picture of what's going on in the Firm in terms of budget, marketing, business development, and so on. Moreover, this sort of active engagement will ensure their commitment to advancing the Firm's goals.

"Wonderful idea. Exposing our best people to the work of running a Firm sounds great theoretically, but what if we—you and I, Bob—don't have the time to adequately explain what to do and how to do it," Mary thoughtfully inquired. "I'm spending way too much time as it is trying to be a responsible mentor to Zuda. Not to mention what happens to the lost billable time for the person who is shadowing us and then stepping up. So Alfred, oh wise one, are you and Joseph prepared to come in once a week for a month and coach Zuda and Piet? Is that how we should spend the additional profits that you helped us to earn?"

"Well, Mary, there you go again. I realize you're skeptical about everything, which is mostly a positive trait," said Alfred with a wink. "Certainly we could be efficient about coaching Zuda and Piet. Their investment in time and your investment in us to do the coaching will pay off rather quickly; they will end up freeing you and Bob to have more billable time on work that you enjoy. They will also create depth in your ranks, so that no one, let me repeat, *no one* is indispensable. I should add that your clients and prospective clients will appreciate this; it shows that there is competent staff available to lead, successfully complete a project, and manage the office in the event of a tragedy. This sort of thoughtfulness is rarely communicated to clients, who would truly value a firm that protects their interests.

2    Andrea Leers, FAIA, in Andrew Pressman, "Good Leadership Helps Practice, the Profession, and Society," *Architectural Record*, September 2007, p. 80.

"Of course, just as you are doing with Zuda, there's a degree of monitoring that has to go with the delegation. You don't want any staffer to feel you've thrown them to the wolves, and you also don't want them mucking things up or overstepping authority. It will be tempting at times to just 'do it yourself' rather than spend the extra time teaching and correcting errors, but in the long run, that's self-defeating as staffers will never learn without the hands-on opportunity.

"You may find that there are some tasks that this or that subordinate is just not inherently capable of handling. There's no sense beating a dead horse in that case. Making such a determination is part of what monitoring is all about.

"When you do find that some of these tasks click into place then the time savings you and Bob are looking for should start to accumulate."

## Client Relations

Here is another excellent point from the planning session that should be implemented tomorrow. Wharton discussed encouraging staff to interact with clients as frequently as possible to enable an appreciation for the rationale for some of the decision-making in addition to the goals of the client and design team. The consequences of this inclusion and resulting deep understanding are a more interesting and ostensibly better project and more employees who feel satisfied in their work. Learning how to listen effectively to clients is another outcome of this approach. (More about collaboration in the section below.)

Personal relationships are critically important to the design process and to the successful completion of a building project. Personal and professional style may vary greatly, and project types may vary greatly, but the one constant in truly successful projects seems to be defined by indelibly etched architect–client relationships. The skill set of the architect must include the ability to choreograph "the give-and-take and the creativity and compromise inherent in any project."[3]

Once again, though, monitoring and teaching are an essential part of the process. Staff needs to understand the limits of authority, as well as what information must stay confidential and what can be shared with clients.

It's also often important that clients do not get the impression that they are being foisted off on junior staff or that they are unimportant to the Principals of the Firm. Certainly, until a client has confidence in the subordinate, there is a definite logic to keeping the senior person on the account well involved in client relations, even if it may mean some duplication. That duplication is just a part of training expense.

---

3  Brian Schermer, AIA, PhD, in Andrew Pressman, *Curing the Fountainheadache: How Architects and Their Clients Communicate*, New York: Sterling, 2006, p. xv.

## Firm Culture

"While we're on the subject of staff," Wharton added, "we must underscore the importance of Firm culture. With such a highly intelligent and talented staff, it behooves you to become entrepreneurial in every sense of the word and to infuse that into the Firm culture. Every employee should have the mandate to identify prospective clients for the Practice.

"The process can start with their own networks of people with like-minded interests and passions. I know this is a cliché, but with hard work and persistence—that is, dedicated time every week or every couple of weeks—a new list of prospects can be developed and nurtured. 'How do you do that?' you may ask. Well it has been our experience that the best way to cultivate a relationship is to *do something good* for the contact (who may indeed have other contacts). It doesn't even have to be professionally relevant as long as it is personally relevant. For example, sending a link to an article on how to make tasty low-fat pizza (together with an article on cool kitchen design), arranging to pick up kids after soccer practice—you get the idea. The point is that this whole effort arises from and is flavored by the individual employee and is a specific expectation of the job from the moment he or she is hired.

"In sum, there is increasing recognition that a firm's cultural environment is a critical factor not only in producing the best possible design work but also in attracting and retaining both new staff *and clients.* Many architectural firms are now including sections on their Web sites dedicated to describing a distinctive office culture and personality."[4]

## Web Site and Social Media

"Speaking of Web sites, yours is rather pathetic, I'm afraid," added Sloan. "It's totally generic; nothing distinctive about it. You could be describing almost any architectural practice almost anywhere in the country. For example, saying, 'We're very service-oriented'—give me a break! Isn't architecture supposed to be a service profession? And I've noticed that the firms who are not known for great design like to emphasize that phrase when, in reality, it's an excuse for dropping the ball on doing their best possible design work—so they can efficiently please the client but not necessarily do their best for the project. They are not mutually exclusive; a professional is supposed to do both."

"Okay, stop, stop . . . we hear you, and we know our Web site is bad," said Bob. "Not that this is a justification, but we delegated the design and unfortunately the content to an intern one summer about three years ago."

"Don't be fooled by those emerging professionals who are very talented and facile with digital technology but don't yet have the experience to make professional judgments about

---

4  Andrew Pressman, "Creating a Firm Culture that Supports Innovative Design," *Architectural Record*, February 2008, p. 65–66.

content and graphic design. Enough with my rant," declared Sloan. "Here's some succinct common-sense conventional wisdom that may help you on the next version of your Web site:

- **Audience.** Who are you targeting? Prospective clients? (If so, what are their character- istics? Are they fairly sophisticated?) Prospective employees? Or both? And what kinds of clients are you targeting—residential, commercial, or government, or all of the above?

- **Content.** What is important to communicate, and equally important, what should you *not* say or show in order to get a personal inquiry, meeting, or whatever your ultimate goal is? Perhaps you just want to pique interest. Communicate your distinctive personality (see 'Firm Culture', above), however that is manifest. Does it include representative work, people, writing/teaching? Does it include meaningful third-party endorsements?

- **Design.** The Web site must reflect excellent design sensibilities; after all, you are selling design services. Both the design of the Web site and the content (graphics, images, writing) must be absolutely *excellent.* And, as with content, the design should reflect the Firm's distinctive personality. (Can you detect a theme here?!)

- **Updating.** Someone must be responsible for this task, and this must occur on a regular basis. Updating is not just changes in and information about the Practice but also keeping up with the technology. For example, does it make sense to have a mobile version that will be user-friendly to mobile phones?"

After a moment's reflection, Mary said, "Thank you for that wake-up call. This is all fairly obvious but frankly we've been so busy and we haven't viewed this as a priority task. We will now; it is our public face.

"Can you shift gears a little bit and talk to us about social media? Honestly, I know we're relatively old—at least Bob is—but it's hard to believe that social media has any significant value for small- to medium-sized professional service firms. Please enlighten us."

Wharton stepped up. "Well, the short answer is that it depends. Alas, nothing is ever straight- forward or simple. Let's go back to basics once again to respond to this. Who is your audience? Who are your prospective clients? Do they surf the Internet to select an architect? Before the Internet, would they have selected an architect from the *Yellow Pages*? Social media may be perfect for homeowners, for example, who are seeking a great fit with an architect and who want to evaluate many portfolios of residential additions and renovations. They may also want to follow architect bloggers and tweeters for the same reason; and the relationship between architect and homeowner is very personal, which is very different from that with institutional clients. So one response, then, in order to bolster the small-scale custom residential arm of your Practice, is to have your work and/or words plastered on billboards all along the information highway.

"But before you do that, first take a step back. It seems like we've justified the hiring of a Marketing Specialist. This person will be tasked to master plan your marketing efforts con- sistent with your new entrepreneurial model and all the soul-searching that generated it (see

Chapter 7). The use of social media and your Web site design will be strategic components—among many others—of that marketing master plan. The best advice I can impart is to hire someone who, of course, has the appropriate knowledge and experience but *who is not generationally biased*. Your prospective client base may be stratified by age, and they may view social media very differently. The marketing person must be sensitive to your clients' demographics and respond accordingly with the appropriate tools, which are constantly evolving."

## COLLABORATION AND BIM

Effective collaboration among architects, consultants, and owners is the single most important ingredient in integrated practice—or any project delivery mode for that matter. Working together well is a meaningful response to the marketplace mandate for complex buildings that are faster to design and construct, at lower cost, as well as more sustainable and of higher quality than those built in the past. A good collaborative environment can facilitate design excellence, a more efficient process, and of course, profitability.

Building Information Modeling (BIM), with its mind-boggling array of features, including energy analyses, building life cycle costs, code compliance checks, coordination and clash detection, rich databases of information, and many others, is promoting a collaborative culture as well. Use of BIM in facilities management is also very appealing to an increasing number of owners who are mandating their architects to use it on their projects.

Especially, but not only, for those who are not regularly in the market for architectural services, if your Practice develops a real expertise in employing this tool, it then also can be used as a marketing tool to educate the client about the prospective value-add that you will be in a position to offer. This can help level the playing field with the larger firms but won't last forever since it is just a matter of time when most everyone will have this capability with technology.

Perhaps the biggest cultural change—and one that Mary and Bob need to address—is not learning how to use new and evolving tools and technology such as BIM but, rather, the attitude adjustment required to collaborate effectively with the entire team from the start (see Figure 8.1). Alas, software by itself has a real downside in that it does not cultivate collaborative engagement among peers; in fact, it tends to discourage it as the computer screen demands absorptive attention to be productive.

Vendor-sponsored tutorials can certainly handle getting up to speed on software, and time should be budgeted for that. But collaborative basics—the soft skills that provide the magic that transforms the most challenging projects into great works of architecture—must be addressed. This too is an area where monitoring, reminding, and intervention play a big role.

Alfred Wharton seized the moment and weighed in on the importance of getting the most out of collaboration by interpreting and synthesizing state-of-the-art insights from business and management worlds as well as precedents from disciplines other than architecture. Talking directly to Mary and Bob, he stated frankly: "You both are so creative and smart that

**Figure 8.1**   Even though a collaborator may be large, shaggy, and have a limited vocabulary, it still behooves the architect to listen actively and to have rapport and respect in order to fully appreciate his or her unique perspectives.

you could actually break new ground on effective collaborative design processes to assist in achieving design excellence and a competitive advantage. Not to mention working effectively cross-culturally and globally and engaging larger-scale projects (see discussion about alliances in Chapter 7)."

"Mary and I fully embrace collaborative work," said Bob, "but how do we get our somewhat self-absorbed, egotistical staff to get on board with this?"

Wharton was thoughtful in his response. "Ah, that's the question. You already have the infrastructure set up with your weekly Friday afternoon wine and cheese event. I recommend that you design a mini-curriculum on collaboration to be delivered at that time. You could invite expert guest speakers, give talks yourselves and have seminars, and equally important, give homework in the form of relevant reading material for discussion.[5] I recommend you assign

---

5   There are some excellent publications on this topic including the second book in the "Designing" trilogy: Andrew Pressman, *Designing Relationships: The Art of Collaboration in Architecture*, Abingdon: Routledge, 2014.

the more arrogant staff—for example, Richard—to present an analysis of some axioms of traditional collaborative dynamics as a means to jump-start the discussion and to ensure their investment. Even if you just assign everyone to come in with a question or a suggestion over some aspect of work relating to the issue, that can be a way to initiate constructive exchanges so that there is a regular collaborative experience that is *personally* relevant.

"Another way to promote a collaborative process is that some firms have their teams review completed projects together to see what could have been done better. Kind of an exit interview as they leave the project. You should seek out opportunities to do this as a matter of course on every project.

"It's important such reviews do not come off as criticism as that's a morale killer and a sure way to end up in arguments over where blame may properly lie. It is true that analyzing failures can be one of the most instructive activities, but it has to be handled with kid gloves, especially if there are different hierarchical levels engaged in the exercise.

"And one final point regarding wine and cheese: asking some of your engineering consultants and selecting current, past, and prospective *clients* to attend your Friday afternoon event could yield enormous benefits. Leveraging this initiative into client relations, marketing, and business development can help justify any investment in speakers, reading material, and time."

"As far as BIM is concerned," Sloan said, now picking up the conversation, "you have to budget for technology. But at the same time you have to realize that the technology is not an end in itself; it's easy to lose sight of the big picture because of the sometimes steep learning curves. There is a lot of flexibility with integrated project delivery and how and when BIM software can be deployed and integrated with other tools and modes of collaboration. I recall your mentioning that not all of your consultants use BIM—that doesn't mean you shouldn't or that you shouldn't hire them.

"Finally I would add that skillful architects have at their disposal a full spectrum of both digital and physical tools and methods, and they recognize that they elicit different dimensions of creativity.[6] We are just scratching the surface here; all of this only begins to suggest the content of your mini-curriculum!"

## SUCCESSION, PRINCIPAL COMPENSATION, AND GETTING PERSONAL

What could be more appropriate to conclude comments on the strategic plan (and the book) than how to gracefully leave the Practice and end the story. But before we discuss

---

6  A book that elaborates on this assertion and provides explicit strategies for doing design is Andrew Pressman, *Designing Architecture: The Elements of Process*, Abingdon: Routledge, 2012.

and resolve the succession plan, we need to address the underlying tension about Mary's and Bob's salaries and bonuses.

## Principals' Goals

Recall from Chapter 2 that the two partners each draw a salary of $82,000, which both feel is insufficiently rewarding. Bob manages the lion's share of administrative tasks and feels he is underappreciated by Mary. Mary is the primary rainmaker for larger projects and thinks she deserves financial recognition for that. Bob brings in work, but his mostly custom residential jobs have much smaller construction budgets and fees than Mary's. Exacerbating the tension are complications in their respective personal lives that each principal has to acknowledge in some way. How should Mary and Bob reconcile their differences to both be fair with annual compensation and the outcome of their succession plan—as Bob is thinking he would retire before Mary?

While catching Mary's eye, Bob began to fill in the context of his personal situation for Sloan and Wharton. "Mary, remember when I was referred to as the 'old man' in design studio back at School? I think I was the only one who was married at that time (to wife #1) and had the beginnings of premature gray hair. At least I wasn't going bald. Yet it was really hard to balance the demands of a family including a 2-year-old child with the total immersion required to be successful as a full-time student in architecture school. In the end, I guess I didn't do such a good job of balancing, as you well know, since I periodically cried on your shoulder for support after the divorce. Then Sally, one of my then firm's clients, came along when I was doing my internship, and our friendship grew as I was working on her little house renovation. A year and a half after that, we were married and have been happily since then, although, quite frankly with alimony and child support payments, we're feeling stressed. We can't just take off and spontaneously go to Paris or London for a long weekend. At this point in my professional career, I feel like I should have the savings to be able to do that—and much more. Maybe I need to retire now and use the money from my share of selling the Practice to move to Europe."

Mary nodded, uncomfortably, and said: "I understand, Bob. I'm pretty happy in my married life now too, but my two girls are a lot younger than your son and daughter. That means I'm facing years of private school tuition times two. Primary school tuition rivals that of many colleges! Needless to say I could put larger bonuses, if not salary, to good use. So, Alfred and Joseph—help! You have clearly been successful in putting us in the right direction to increase revenue and profits and to decrease overhead. Can you offer some suggestions about how to fairly divide the available wealth between us?"

Sloan began answering. "Mary, it's great that you used that word *wealth* in your question because it encompasses much more than just current income. Part of that wealth is your stake in ownership in the Practice. When Bob talks about selling, he's talking about converting that stake into cash in one way or another.

"I know you two have discussed succession planning in the context of Firm culture, and you seem to both recognize how a smart plan can be so much more than just a schedule for transferring ownership. For example, the succession plan in the back of your minds was clearly a part of the inspiration for the idea to rotate administrative roles among worthy staff to expose them to Firm leadership and to prepare them for eventually becoming principals and hopefully taking over the Firm to make that cash conversion possible for both of you. As and if these high-potential staff prove themselves, awareness of their career trajectory that culminates in ownership and leadership can facilitate their loyalty and can provide the motivation to contribute to all aspects of the Firm's success.

"We recognize that Bob is seven years older than Mary, and Bob says he is interested in moving overseas within the next few years so it seems clear that he will retire earlier than Mary. The conventional wisdom is that planning for a smooth transition of both the leadership and ownership ought to begin as much as ten years prior to retirement of a principal as it is believed to take that long to cultivate the appropriate skills, transfer the responsibilities and contacts in the marketplace, develop close client relationships, provide the best mentorship, and so on.

"Let's start with the present and with the basics. These two questions, current income and long-term succession, are intertwined.

"I'll turn to Bob's side of the coin (no pun intended) first. What's your timetable, Bob? How many years do you want to keep working? As you answer that question, the next question is how much do you feel you need to get out of your stake in the Practice in order to be able to live the post-M&B life you're thinking of?

"The Breakeven Analysis tool we provided gives you a way to model out over that period of years what the Practice can produce in profits. However, rather than focus on one model output, I'd consider a range of outputs because of the uncertainty about the future. With your experience, you and Mary can probably be pretty confident in the range of projections you settle upon.

"Now, part of that question goes back to another tool we talked about, which is cash flow. As you gauge that range of projections, one of the inputs you have to deal with is capacity and the funding of capacity. The more money you take out of the Practice on a current basis, the less you have readily available to fund the growth I know you need to yield the kind of outcome you want. Furthermore, the more you take out in the short run, the less valuable the stake in the Practice will be in the long run.

"Conceptually, this analysis is like any other investment in securities. There are three and only three sources of benefit from any enterprise, and their sum over a defined period of expectation determines the worth of the investment at any particular moment in time:

1. Current income;

2. Tax benefits (which, of course, can be negative);

3. Cash-out.

"Take out too much cash too early and you hinder or even cripple the ability to adequately grow the cash-out portion of the return; plus the more you take, the greater the chance that the marginal current income dollar will be less beneficial on an after-tax basis. Don't or can't take out enough and your anxiety to cash out—to get out—increases exponentially. Got to find a happy medium.

"One key question in that medium is what is the value? There are a fair number of valuation formulas and theories for justifying each. One rule of thumb is a percentage of the most recent year's Practice revenues or of a three- or five-year average. That percentage tends to shift over time with changes in interest rates and other financial market rates of return. In any event, it's rare that a practice will be worth more than one year's worth of revenues, and numbers like 50% to 80% may well be applicable in various economic circumstances.

"You may think that's not very much and you may be right. Part of the reason is that for professional practices, most everything depends on the professional. If there is more than one owner then control is divided and dilution of control creates risks. As risks increase, value drops. The bonds of an issuer with a bad credit rating are worth less than those of an issuer with a good credit rating.

"Lastly, it's important to keep in mind that the cash-out has to come from somewhere. Who's going to pay for the intrinsic value of the stake? The cost has to be affordable to a buyer; otherwise there's nothing else to do but close the Practice and accept the minimal liquidating value for whatever the saleable assets will bring at that time less any liabilities. More than a few practices realize that disappointing fate."

It was Wharton's turn to pick up the thread. "Now, on Mary's side of the coin, ultimately there are two transitions to face. The first is Bob leaving and the second is her own retirement out there at some later date.

"For the first, she might be the buyer of Bob's interest or have the Practice be the buyer, which is the same thing in terms of end result. There might be different tax advantages or different financing opportunities one way or the other. Alternatively, someone else may be the buyer, in which case she has to be able to survive and prosper with a substitute co-owner. Getting the chemistry right, on both a professional and personal basis, can be a tall order, particularly if the newbie is a stranger. If it's an insider, a current employee, there's the potential strain of morphing the entrenched relationship of superior to subordinate into one of equals or, if not exactly equals, one in which the subordinate has a practical form of veto power, whether or not that power is legally reserved. On the second, Mary's planning template is no different than Bob's, though the contents are sure to vary to a greater or lesser degree.

"Fundamentally, the key to any plan toward reaching your goals, joint or individual, is going to have to be better economic performance of the Firm itself. We think if you wisely and effectively employ the tools we've given you and exercise refined and improving business judgment, you can achieve that.

"So let's return to the first half of the question, that of current income. Since you both own half the Company, you each have a legal right to half the profit. It is possible to say that one or the other of you should have a higher salary or a greater bonus that gets subtracted and paid before the profits are considered for division. It's not our place to make that call and, in fact, it would be a violation of our ethics to even consider such a question to the advantage or disadvantage of just one of you.

"I will say that if you both agreed that there were disparities in the benefits the Practice was obtaining from each of you and you wanted to pursue that line of thinking, we'd recommend that rather than making some kind of artificial assignment of incomes, you set up your own metrics—much like the incentive compensation plan we talked about for staff—and let those results determine income. If you do that, we'd urge you to consider a value for administrative activities because, if there is none, the incentive will be to ignore accounting, human resources, overhead cost controls, etc., and that will land you right back where you are now or maybe even in worse shape.

"It is fair to say, though, that exactly that kind of question has led to the breakup of innumerable practices, indeed businesses of all kinds. Sometimes that's to the regret of all; sometimes not. You each have to consider yourselves and your families. If you believe you are going to be better off apart, or even if just one of you does, then a different kind of consultant is needed to help you break up with as little pain as possible. And, by the way, if we thought the future for M&B was bleak, we'd tell you that. As our analysis has proceeded you can see that does not appear to be the case."

Mary and Bob both smiled. Those smiles were really all that were needed to answer the question, but each of them still said, quite emphatically, that the whole looked like it would be much greater than the sum of the parts.

"OK, then," said Sloan. "What's needed, in my opinion, is to set a reasonable goal for current income for yourselves and run that through the models to see what you need to do to get that current yield. Assuming you can do it, when and if you can start to throw off some material excess cash, there are several concepts that you may want to examine for building the value for the other half of the question, the succession plan, which might just as easily be called the cash-out.

"One device you might think about is using life insurance to build up a fund to help create the wealth you are each looking for. A buy-sell plan funded with life insurance provides protection for the families in the event of the untimely death of one of you. (Is it ever really timely?) If you both live, the cash value in the policy might be accessed to facilitate the retirement transition—maybe by being converted to an annuity, maybe by being cashed in, or maybe used in some other manner. There are different kinds of policies that build value and lots of variations in terms for how the policies can be managed.

"We all agree there's nobody on staff who is a certainty for ownership, but there are some prospects. Nurturing those prospects and carefully drawing out their intentions, and perhaps those of employees-to-be as they come aboard, may be another building block. I say 'carefully draw out' because I've heard some horror stories about lawsuits claiming promises of ownership were made. Your lawyer should be able to give you some advice on how to approach the question.

"If you do decide there is someone or more than one with potential then you might try to make the transition in stages, bringing the junior or juniors into minority ownership with the possibility of expansion of their shares as time goes on. Decisions and processes are then needed to establish and re-establish how control and rights change with each increment in such a gradual approach. That gradualism may, itself, be viewed as a benefit.

"Another approach is to build a fund through savings and investment that the Firm owns to utilize in the buyout. That may have some tax aspects to it that don't work well, depending on the overall combined tax profiles of the Firm and its owners, but it may be worth examining.

"Another method that has some unique tax characteristics is that of establishing an Employee Stock Ownership Plan (an ESOP) when the time is right. In essence, that involves a transfer of ownership to a trust, in which all employees have a stake. As employees come and go, their interest in the Firm is acquired or liquidated through the trust. Such arrangements often have a financing element, making an ESOP attractive to owners, as the entity effectively collateralizes itself. Beware, though, because that collateral is almost always accompanied with the retiring owner's personal guarantee, so it's imperative the entity continues to prosper.

"Let's also not forget that the possibility may be out there for the Practice to be acquired by a larger architectural firm. That might occur in such a way that Bob then retires while Mary continues in practice with the acquirer. You can imagine the other possibilities. Of course, for that to happen, there has to be both value and synergy, which tend to complement one another.

"In any event, focus on both the present *and* the future, which are so inextricably linked, to use these tools and capitalize on the opportunity that seems to be out there for you to jointly seize."

At its best, succession planning is a valuable part of practice and integral to Firm culture. Viewed strategically, it can support recruiting, developing, and advancing the best people as well as rewarding the retiring principals in multiple ways.

## FINAL WORDS

"It's truly been a pleasure working with you," said Joseph Sloan. "We've done everything we can to underscore the importance of thinking of business matters as so well integrated with everything that you do on a daily basis that they become almost second nature. And the primary way of accomplishing that is to view *everything* as a design problem—not just your projects. In that way, and with the requisite background we have provided, you can unleash the power of your creative design thinking toward solving myriad vexing and wicked problems that confront all of us in the design profession and construction industry—*and* enjoy the challenges!"

# INDEX